How Much Time Has God Given This World?

How Much Time Has God Given This World?

You need to know Because the Bible Says we are living in the Last Generation

*A*dvantage
BOOKS

Charles Kenneth

Library of Congress Catalog Number: 2019936094
REL012040 RELIGION/ Christian Living / Inspirational
REL006730 RELIGION / Biblical Studies / Old Testament

First Printing: May 2019
19 20 21 22 23 24 25   10 9 8 7 6 5 4 3
Printed in the United States of America

Table of Contents

Preface

Why read this book? That is a good question and deserves a good answer. Anytime we chose to read a book, we are choosing to take a portion of the finite amount of time that God has given us on this earth to read it. The time it takes to read the book is time that could have been spent doing something else and since we only have a certain amount of time on earth, we should not take those decisions lightly.

God's Word, the Bible, says we are living in the last generation before Jesus Christ will return (see chapter 1) and take all those who truly believe in Jesus as their only source of salvation back to heaven with Him. The event where Jesus will come to take His true believers back to heaven with Him is called the Rapture (chapter 2). All those who will be taken in the Rapture (chapters 3 and 4) will stay in heaven until they return to earth with Jesus after God pours out His wrath on an unbelieving world over the next seven years (chapter 6). According to God's Word, all these events are going to begin happening soon (chapter 5) and they are <u>guaranteed</u> to happen as all previous predictions in the Bible up to this point in history have come true (see Introduction).

You don't want to miss the Rapture and be left on earth when God pours out His wrath.

<u>That</u> is why you need to read this book.

This book is the result of something that I went looking for (to invest my time in) but could not find. A book that would give me, not only a better idea of how much time God has given this world before the Rapture might occur, but also a very detailed description of what the world will be like after the removal of all true believers in Jesus Christ. I wanted to learn more about the times both before and after the Rapture so I could tell (and warn) others about it, and I also wanted a book I could give to unbelieving family and friends and could say, "Even if you don't choose to read this now, keep it. You will be so glad you did if you are left here on earth and God starts pouring out His wrath on an unbelieving world."

I was not looking for a book that takes God's truth about what will happen before, during and after the Rapture, combine it with fictional characters and reveal it through story. That has already been done several times before. Those stories are good, but in order to develop the characters and tell a story, they require limiting the amount of information I was looking for. I wanted a book that would give me as much information as possible, laid out in a combination of narrative, bullet point and other lists, and then let God's direction and my imagination take it from there.

No two person's imagination will paint the same picture, and with a book like that, I believe God will most certainly use His Holy Spirit in a way that will be very effective at convincing people they need to take Jesus Christ as Lord and Savior. Either when reading the book before the Rapture occurs, or after when they witnessed the most earth-shattering event of their lives and they better figure out why they were left behind. However, God pouring out His wrath *after* the Rapture will be even more earth-shattering, I assure you.

After searching online for a book like that, and not being able to find it, I decided to write it. That decision was not made lightly. Writing a book takes a lot of time both to research and to write, and after it was written, how could I be certain someone would publish it? Believe me, there was a lot of prayer beforehand as I knew such a project without God's blessing for knowledge, wisdom, time, and a publisher would go nowhere. However, after reviewing where God had me at this point in my life, it seemed like He had been preparing me to write this book from a long time ago and I didn't even know it until now. The book is in your hand so I believe God gave me His blessing to write it.

My prayer is that you will be moved to read this book. It makes me feel so much better knowing many of my family members and friends (and now you) have the book to understand what is happening in the world now, and also the things that will happen soon. If you are reading this book before the Rapture has occurred and do not have faith in the life, death and resurrection of Jesus Christ for the salvation of your soul, I pray this book moves you to reconsider.

If the Rapture has already occurred and you're reading this book to find out what happened and to figure out why you were not taken, my prayer is that you get saved first! Go to chapter 6 where the book talks about what happens after the Rapture and read about what *already has happened* and please consider praying the prayer there (or one like it) and become saved. Your salvation is what matters most. Don't wait another minute. Then you can go back and read the first part of the book about who was taken, who was not, and why.

If you are not a Christian, I'm quite aware that I have already used words that may not be familiar to you. Turn the page for a better description of some of those words and also to explain how God prepared me to write this book. This will help you make that all-important decision whether you invest some of the time God has given you on this earth to read it; or at the very least to save it for after the Rapture. Hint – It will help you whether you are a believer or not.

Introduction

The first thing we need to establish is the Bible's credibility to be believed. I mentioned to you that every prophecy written in the Bible has come true up to this point in history, and that is correct. It is beyond the scope of this book to give you proof after proof of that, but I will give you the best one and you can follow up yourself after that. There is absolutely no doubt there was a man who lived named Jesus Christ, who claimed to be God, who did miracles, who was executed on a cross by the Roman governor at that time, Pontius Pilate, and He was seen alive again after his death. Many historians say the evidence for the resurrection of Jesus Christ is better authenticated than just about anything that has happened in all of history. If you are thinking, "Well, that's just what the Bible says," I have news for you. Everything I told you there came from historical sources outside the Bible. (1)

Where the Bible comes into this is that it contains over 100 specific prophecies written about Jesus by men called prophets, and even though they were written hundreds (and some of them thousands) of years before Jesus was born, He fulfilled every single prophecy. A mathematician once calculated the probability of one person fulfilling just eight of those prophecies would be one in 10 to the 17th power. That is a 1 with 17 zeroes after it. If you had that many silver dollars, you could cover the entire state of Texas to a depth of two feet. (2)

The probability of one person fulfilling 48 of the prophecies was calculated to be one in 10 to the 157th power. (3) That is more than the number of atoms (10 to the 80th power) which are estimated to be in the known universe. (4)

Want to see what the chances of one person fulfilling 48 of the prophecies written about Jesus in the Bible looks like written out?

1 person in 10,000,000,000,000,000,000,000,000,000,000,000,00 0,000,000,000,000, 000,000,000,000,000,000,000,000,000 (number of atoms estimated to be in known universe stops here), 000,000,000,000,000,000,000,000,000,000,000,000,000,000,00 0,000,000, 000,000,000,000,000,000

However, Jesus didn't just fulfill 48 of the prophecies, He fulfilled them all (Luke 24:44). What do you think the chances were of that? The number of zeroes in that calculation would probably take up a whole page (or more), but Jesus did it. If ever there was a reason to believe what is written in the Bible is true, Jesus fulfilling over 100 specific prophecies about Himself written hundreds of years before He was born is it, and God said He put those prophecies in the Bible by inspiring men to write what He wanted them to write through His Holy Spirit (2 Peter 1:20-21).

I gave you a couple of references to verses in the Bible and you are going to be seeing a lot more of them. There are a few reasons for that, but the main one is this – Don't take my word for what I'm telling you, take God's Word for it. There are many things written in this book that need to be backed up by God's Word and since this book is written for both believers and non-believers, if there is any doubt that whatever is being said may not be believed or understood, then a reference to where to find it in the Bible will be added. The other reason for using a lot of Bible verses is because that is what I looked for in the books I chose to read in preparing to write this book. The Bible says all of God's Word is useful for teaching (2 Timothy 3:16), so if I am going to read something that I want to learn from and pass on to others, then that is the basis that I'm going to use for this book too.

Now I mentioned before that God had been preparing me to write this book for years and I didn't even know it, and that is true. Over the past ten plus years, in addition to studying God's Word almost every day, I have read over 120 books in an effort to increase in knowledge and wisdom of what God reveals about Himself, Jesus, the Holy Spirit, and what is written in the Bible. Understanding this is important because you may have noticed there is no 'Dr.' or 'Pastor' in front of my name. Therefore, I should establish my credentials and describe how God prepared me to write this book.

I have completed a year and a half of studies and became a licensed lay deacon in my church district of California, Nevada and Hawaii. I also have an insatiable desire to grow in knowledge and wisdom of God, Jesus, the Holy Spirit, and God's Word the Bible. However, the main reason I think God was preparing me for years to write this book is I most enjoy learning about the end times as revealed in the Bible. I have always gravitated towards that part of God's Word and have a higher percentage of those kinds of books in my library. I hope that helps give you a better idea about myself and why I feel God gave me His blessing to pursue a book of this kind.

The first part of this book establishes why we are living in the last generation before Jesus returns, what the Rapture is, the promises of God showing that the Rapture <u>will</u> occur, and who will be taken, who will not, and why. The middle part of the book discusses the timing of the Rapture, provides some answers to the title/question on the cover, and the last part will go over what will happen after the Rapture; after God removes hundreds of millions of people from the world in the blink of an eye. The book then finishes with some (but by no means all) of the wonderful promises from the Bible for those saved through faith in Jesus alone. All of this will be backed up by many references to proofs found in God's Word.

There will be many Bible verses given, but it may be up to you to look them up in a Bible. The reason for that is two-fold. First, in order to conserve space in the book to provide as much information as possible about why this is the last generation before the Rapture, the timing of when the Rapture might occur, who will be taken, who will not, and why, as well as what will happen after the Rapture. Secondly, and just as important, is because any time you open a Bible and look inside, God is liable to show you something you wouldn't have seen otherwise.

Regarding the last chapter that talks about what will happen after the Rapture occurs, I realize many people may in fact read it <u>after</u> the Rapture. Bibles may be hard to find after the Rapture and they will become very hard to find the closer it gets to the end of the world, so for that reason, most of the verses will be provided for you in the last chapter. Faith comes from hearing (or reading) God's Word (Romans 10:17), so I want to make sure most of the verses are included if a Bible is not available.

There also will be an appendix at the end of the book for further study on many of the things that are discussed, as I know there will be those that may want more examples from God's Word, or because a statement was made which should have more details to back it up. Writing to an audience that could include everyone from an atheist who doesn't believe in God to someone who has been a Christian their whole life (and everyone in-between) means some will want to read more on certain parts of God's Word, but others will feel like it is not necessary for their understanding.

The appendix is there to give every reader more explanation if they choose to investigate and learn a bit more. There you will also find some resources I would recommend for further study. I point out when we cannot the take time (space in the book) to go into more detail on some of the things that are said, but will refer you to the appendix and those other resources if you want to learn more.

Finally, this book was written with a sense of urgency. For non-believers, it is imperative that you read this book in as little time as possible and make a decision as to whether you believe in salvation through faith in Jesus Christ or not because the Rapture could happen very soon. Even if you do not have any understanding of the Bible, you should be able to read through the book without consulting the appendix and still have enough information to see the truth of God's Word. For those who are already true believers, this book will give you a much better understanding of what is coming soon so that you will have a better idea of what to do with the time you have left; to witness to those whom God has called you to be a witness.

Ok, time to learn about why God's Word says this is the last generation on earth before Jesus returns, what the Rapture is, and what it will do to the world. The wonderful blessing that the Rapture will be for God's true believers who will be taken, and the devastating effects it will have on the world and for those who are not taken.

Ready?

Turn the page.

1

The Last Generation

The Bible really does say we are living in the last generation before Jesus returns and the ramifications of that are enormous. If you thought you had a certain amount of time left on this earth, but then found out it was not as much time as you thought you had, wouldn't that change the way you lived the rest of your life?

We see this happen all the time as we get closer to the average life expectancy in this world of 66 years for men and 69 years for women (in America it is 76 years for men and 81 years for women). As we get closer to when we might die, it changes the way we live and life takes on new meaning. Why wouldn't it? As we get closer to the death of our bodies, it makes sense that we would live the remainder of our lives differently than if we felt like we had more time left.

However, what if you thought you had more time but didn't? Anyone who has lived any amount of time in this world knows the next day or next month or next year is not guaranteed. The Bible says none of us should presume we will be alive in a year or <u>even a day</u> from now, because the fact is, we simply don't know (James 4:13-16). God knows when each of us will die (Psalm 139:16), but we do not. So, when God's Word the Bible says we are living in the last generation before Jesus returns, and that we do not have as much time as we thought we had, this is something that we should make every effort to understand.

When Jesus came to Jerusalem for the last time before He would be crucified, He told His disciples that the temple in Jerusalem would eventually be destroyed and not one stone would remain on top of the other (Matthew 24:2). His disciples' response to that prophecy was this –

"Tell us, when will all this happen? What will signal your return and the end of the world?" – Matthew 24:3

Jesus then told them all these things would happen in the last days, leading up to His return –

- Many will come claiming to be the Messiah (Matthew 24:5)
- You will hear of wars and threats of wars (verse 6)
- There will be famines and pestilences and earthquakes (verse 7, NKJV)
- Christians will be hated all over the world (verse 9)
- Many false prophets will appear and deceive many (verse 11)
- Sin will be rampant everywhere (verse 12)
- The love of many will grow cold (verse 12)

Can anyone say all these things are not happening more now than at any time in history?

- In the 18th century there were two people who claimed to be the Messiah Jesus, in the 19th century there were six people who made the same claim, in the 20th century there were fourteen people, and after only twenty years into in the 21st century there are ten (one died in 2009) who claim they are the Messiah Jesus (1)
- We read of current wars and rumors of more wars all the time today
- In 2019, 842 million people in the world didn't have enough to eat (2)
- The coronavirus has become the most feared pestilence the world has ever seen
- There have been 269 earthquakes magnitude 7.0 or higher in the past twenty years and 23 higher than 8.0 compared to only 6 that were 8.0 or higher in the 1990's (3)
- Every five minutes a Christian is killed for their faith (4)
- Many false prophets have appeared and deceived billions (see appendix for examples)
- Would take a whole book to cover the increase of sin in the world
- Self-centeredness has become the norm in the last generation

Now these things do not prove we are living in the last generation before Jesus returns, but they do give us a very good indication that we are; they fulfill all the things He said would happen during the last generation of this world. Jesus then followed up everything he told His disciples about His coming again with this statement –

"Now learn a lesson from the fig tree. When it's branches bud and its leaves begin to sprout, you know that summer is near. In the same way, when you see all these things, you can know His (Jesus') return is very near, right at the door. I tell you the truth, this generation will not pass from the scene until all these things take place." – Matthew 24:32-34

Many skeptics have used this passage to say the prophecies of Him returning to earth are false because that generation from Jesus' time (and many more) have come and gone but Jesus has not returned yet. However, Jesus was not talking about the generation that was alive at that time when He said that. We know this is true because Jesus had already said that the kingdom of God would be taken away from that generation because they did not believe in Him (Matthew 21:43).

Jesus said when the branches of the fig tree bud, and its leaves begin to sprout, you will know His return is very near. The key here is identifying what the fig tree represents because once that 'fig tree' starts to blossom, then that will identify the last generation that Jesus was talking about that will not pass away before He returns again.

So, what does the fig tree represent?

The fig tree represents the nation of Israel.

Jesus once told this story –

"A man had a fig tree growing in his vineyard, and he went to look for fruit on it but did not find any. So he said to the man who took care of the vineyard, 'For three years now I've been coming to look for fruit on this fig tree and haven't found any. Cut it down! Why should it use up the soil?' – Luke 13:6-7, NIV

This story is referring to Jesus' ministry on earth, which lasted three years (discussed in chapter 5). The fig tree is the nation of Israel, and Jesus spent three years ministering to them. He told the people that He was the Messiah spoken of from the Old Testament (Luke 4: 16-21, John 4:25-26), looked for the resulting fruit that would have occurred on the fig tree Israel if they believed Him, but at the end of those three years, Jesus took the kingdom away from Israel because they did not believe Him (Matthew 21:43). The fig tree Israel was eventually cut down when

Jerusalem was destroyed in 70AD, and Israel ceased to be a nation for nearly 1900 years.

So, when Jesus answered His disciples' question about when He would return again, Jesus said it will be –

When you see many people are falsely claiming to be the Messiah, hearing of wars and rumors of more wars, increasing famines, pestilences, and earthquakes, worldwide persecution of Christians, many false prophets appearing that claim a different way to be saved that deceives possibly billions unto damnation, rampant sin everywhere, people's hearts growing cold towards one another, and the fig tree Israel has become a nation again. Then, you will know the summer (the season of His return) is near, and the generation that sees all these things happening will not pass away before Jesus returns again.

Israel became a nation again on May 14th 1948, in a miracle foretold by God (Isaiah 66:8-9), in one day, just as God said would happen (verse 8).

God's Word says the birth of a child is considered the beginning of a generation (Matthew 1:2-17), so the generation of Israelites born from the time Israel became a nation again is the last generation that will not pass away before Jesus returns.

I suppose it is possible Jesus was referring to any child born since May 14th, 1948 as being part of the last generation, and not just of those born in Israel. However, since Jesus entrusted the revelation of salvation through faith in Him to the nation of Israel first (Romans 3:2), and Jesus was speaking only to Israel when He was on earth (Matthew 15:24), and Jesus is not done with Israel (as some teach) since God made them a nation again according to His prophetic Word (Isaiah 66:8-9); it is much more likely that Jesus was referring only to the last generation of Israelites that would be born from the time Israel became a nation again.

Now that we understand this extremely important information given to us from God's Word, we need to find out the amount of time that constitutes the last generation according to God. We are fond of giving names to generations and everyone has a different interpretation of how many years make up a generation. However, the only thing that matters now is the amount of time that God says makes up that generation, because we need to know how long that is.

The Bible gives a few examples of how long God considers a generation to be, from forty years (Numbers 32:13), to eighty years (Psalm 90:10), to one hundred years (Genesis 15:13,16), but since there has been more than forty years since Israel became a nation again, we can know it will be one of the remaining two.

Here is the reference in God's Word to a generation being eighty years –

"Seventy years are given to us! Some even live to eighty." – Psalm 90:10

Here is the reference to a generation being one hundred years –

"Then the Lord said to Abram, 'You can be sure that your descendants will be strangers in a foreign land, where they will be oppressed as slaves for 400 years...After four generations your descendants will return here to this land..." – Genesis 15:13,16

This means that if a generation is at most 100 years, then according to Jesus, His return should be by the year 2048 at the latest. However, I would argue that it is probably eighty years for the generation Jesus was referring to, and will point out in chapter 5 why I believe that to be the case. I will explain how, when taken as a whole, and with many examples from God's Word, eighty years makes more sense.

Now I would like to mention here, the Bible does say people used to live to be hundreds of years old from the time God made the first man and woman, Adam and Eve, and that's true. God says the oldest person to ever live was Methuselah at 969 years of age (Genesis 5:27), and while that seems unbelievable to us now, don't forget we were originally created by God to live forever! (Genesis 2:15)

There are many things contributing to much shorter life spans now compared to then. The greatest reason we don't live as long now is because sin has corrupted our DNA and brought death (Romans 6:23); and over the last 6000 years (see chapter 5 for timeframe) our DNA has become worse and shortened our lives. In addition, the earth also fell with man's sin (Genesis 3:17-18, Romans 8:20-22) which caused the atmosphere, as well as the food, that used to help sustain longer lives to deteriorate over time too.

There are many reasons why we don't live as long as we used to, but it doesn't matter how long a generation lived thousands of years ago. What matters is how long a generation lives today. Specifically, how long the last generation that Jesus was referring to will live - The generation that began when Israel became a nation again in 1948.

Now turn the page to get a better understanding about God's promises found in the Bible regarding how, and why, Jesus will return to take millions and millions of true believers back to heaven with Him. Also to get a better idea of what will happen to the rest of world after He does.

2

What is the Rapture?

We must begin by establishing what the Rapture is and what is the reason for the Rapture. The Rapture is a promise given by God in several places in the Bible and specifically mentioned by Jesus in the book of John, chapter 14, verses 2 and 3, where He will come down from heaven at some point in the future and take all His true believers still alive on earth back to heaven with Him. The reason He will do this is because God promises that those who truly believe in Jesus as their only way to be saved are not appointed to His wrath (1 Thessalonians 1:10), but to receive salvation through faith in Jesus Christ (1 Thessalonians 5:9) and thus will not have to be on the earth when God pours out His wrath on an unbelieving world (Revelation 3:10).

The time when God will pour out His wrath on the world is called the Tribulation, and it will last seven years. There are other names for those seven years in the Bible, such as the hour of trial or hour of testing (as described in Revelation 3:10), but it is generally known as the Tribulation. The Rapture is considered a blessed hope by Christians (Titus 2:13) because it will happen before the Tribulation takes place, and will be the event that saves them from having to be on earth when God unleashes His 21 judgments on the world (described in the last chapter of this book).

Three 'main' passages in the Bible talk about what the Rapture is and that it will take place. I already gave you the one from Jesus in John chapter 14. The other two come from the apostle Paul in letters written to the churches at Thessalonica and Corinth. Let's look at all three passages in their context.

The first one came from Jesus the day before He was arrested and crucified. He and His disciples had finished the Last Supper and Jesus then talked to them about many things, one of them was that He would return at some point in the future to take all true believers still alive on earth back to heaven with Him –

"In my Father's house (in heaven) are many dwelling places; if it were not so, I would have told you; for I go to prepare a place for you. If I go to

prepare a place for you, I will come again and receive you to Myself, that where I am (in heaven), there you may be also." John 14:2-3 – NASB

Jesus gave them this promise to help comfort them because He would be taken away from them that very evening and crucified the next day. They replied by asking Him where He was going and how could they know the way to follow?

His response to them was –

"I am the way, the truth and the life. No one can come to the Father except through me." – John 14:6

There are other verses in the Bible that say Jesus is the only way to be saved for eternal life. They are – John 17:3, Acts 4:12, Romans 5:1, 9-10, 1 Corinthians 15:21-22, 2 Corinthians 5:18-19, 1 Timothy 2:5, Hebrews 9:27-28 and Revelation 1:18 to name a few. But in John 14:6, Jesus was responding to a question by saying if you want to be taken back to heaven when He comes (at the Rapture), believing in Him is the only way.

Now I know many believers have not considered John 14:2-3 a Rapture verse before, and those not familiar with the Rapture certainly would not be able to make the connection. Generally, those words spoken by Jesus are interpreted to be when Jesus comes back to set foot on the earth again, but these are two separate events.

The Bible says that when Jesus comes back and sets foot on the earth again, He will bring all those in heaven with Him (Revelation 19:14). This means if there is going to be a future event where Jesus is going to come and take all true believers back to heaven with Him, it cannot be when He returns to earth. It must be when He comes 'in the clouds' (not going all the way down to earth), and this is what we see happening in the second of these three main passages in the Bible regarding the Rapture.

It was written to the church in Thessalonica by the apostle Paul who established that church during one of his missionary journeys through the Roman Empire. The people there were undergoing such severe persecution for their faith in Jesus that they thought they had missed His return. In response, Paul told them this –

"For since we believe that Jesus died and was raised to life again, we also believe that when Jesus returns (as predicted by Jesus in John 14:3), God will bring back with Him (to heaven) the believers who have died. We

tell you this directly from the Lord Jesus: We who are still living when the Lord returns will not meet Him ahead of those who have died. For the Lord Himself will come down from heaven with a commanding shout, with the voice of the archangel, and the trumpet call of God. First, the believers who have died will rise from their graves. Then, together with them, we who are still alive and remain on the earth will be caught up in the clouds to meet the Lord in the air. Then we will be with the Lord forever." – 1 Thessalonians 4:13-17

This passage says nothing about Jesus setting foot on the earth and cannot be referring to when He will come back to earth again. It is saying that when He returns 'in the clouds', He will rapture His true believers back to heaven with Him and fulfill His promise made in John 14:3. There are a few other things from these words in Thessalonians that also tell us this cannot be when Jesus returns to set foot on the earth again.

Paul says when this event he is speaking of takes place (when Jesus returns 'in the clouds'), all true believers in Christ that have died will be raised from the dead *before* all the other believers who are still alive will be taken.

There are Scriptures in Revelation that talk about Jesus coming back to set foot on the earth again, but those Scriptures say the believers that will be raised from the dead will be raised *after* He has set up His thousand-year kingdom (Revelation 20: 4-6). The Scriptures in Revelation also say those who will be resurrected after Jesus comes back to set foot on the earth again will only be the believers that were killed during the seven-year Tribulation. This passage in Thessalonians is talking about the Rapture, not Jesus' return to the earth. They are two separate events.

Now the third main passage regarding the Rapture comes from 1 Corinthians 15:51-50. The apostle Paul is writing to the church in Corinth, which he also established during one of his missionary journeys, and this whole chapter deals with God resurrecting the dead. First Paul talks about the resurrection of Christ, assuring the believers in Corinth that Christ was raised from the dead, gives some proofs for it, and adds that if Christ was not raised from the dead, no one will be raised from the dead and all believers would still be unforgiven of their sins (1 Corinthians 15:17-18).

After Paul gives more reasons and proofs that Christ was raised from the dead, he tells the believers at Corinth a 'secret' regarding the Rapture.

"But let me reveal to you a wonderful secret. We will not all die, but we will be transformed! It will happen in a moment, in the blink of an eye, when the last trumpet is blown. For when the trumpet sounds, those who have died will be raised to live forever, and we who are living will also be transformed." – 1 Corinthians 15:50-51

There are several similarities between this passage and the one in Thessalonians that would indicate Paul is talking about the Rapture and not when Jesus comes to set foot on the earth again. First, the order of the resurrection is the same as in the passage from Thessalonians. The dead are raised first, then the other believers still alive are changed. We already saw that this order of events does not happen when Jesus sets foot on the earth again. The other thing we see here that indicates Paul is talking about the Rapture is when Jesus does finally set foot on the earth again, He does not give all the other believers still alive on earth their resurrection bodies until after His thousand-year reign is completed (Revelation 20:7-9).

We already established the number one reason why you should believe what is written in the Bible is true. That is because Jesus fulfilled over 100 prophecies about Himself that were written hundreds of years before He was born. Also, everything else written in the Bible about other events of history has come true up to this point. So, if the Bible has been 100% accurate up to this point, it will be 100% accurate about what it says will happen from this point on. The Rapture included! Therefore, I implore you to believe that the Rapture *will* occur, and to receive the gift of God's grace through faith in Jesus alone before it does and be taken.

This is as much space as we will devote to what the Rapture is and where some of the proofs for it can be found in God's Word. For those of you that want more detail and explanations about the Rapture, see the references at the end of the book for other sources that go into more detail about what we discussed in this chapter.

3

How Many Will Be Taken in the Rapture?

So how many will be taken in the Rapture? That is a question that cannot be answered with absolute certainty as only God knows who has truly received the offer of His saving grace (2 Timothy 2:19). However, we can study God's Word and based on what it says, make a good guess. To begin, let's try to set a good place to start, as I have seen estimates as high as several billion of the current world's adult population. Based on even a few of the words of Jesus in the Bible, it won't be that many. Let's look into God's Word for a better estimate.

The best place to start would probably be something from God's Word that could give us a good idea of how many people will find eternal life over the entire course of history. A good guess, as far as a percentage goes, of all the people who have ever lived on earth that will inherit eternal life. From this, we will take many more examples from God's Word and refine it even more. Then that 'percentage' we come up with could be used as a reasonable estimate to how many still alive might be taken in the Rapture too. To do this, an excellent place to start would be from Matthew chapter 7, verses 13 and 14.

"You can enter God's kingdom only through the narrow gate. The highway to hell is broad, and its gate is wide for the many who choose that way. But the gateway to life is very narrow and the road is difficult, and only a few ever find it."

Based on this passage of God's Word, what percentage of people do you think that would be? The key words here are 'broad' describing the road and 'wide' describing the gate needed for those who will not choose to receive God's grace. Versus 'difficult' describing the road and 'narrow' describing gate for entering into God's kingdom. In addition, to make sure no one misses the point, Jesus says only a few ever find that gate. So, what do you think that percentage would that be? Twenty-five? Twenty? Less? I think it's safe to say that would be less than twenty percent, but let's go deeper into God's Word and come up with a better guess than that.

Let's start with a list of what God's Word says regarding beliefs and traits of those who are true believers, and thus would be taken at the Rapture. This list is by no means all-encompassing; it is only a partial list. The verses shown to back up what is said are not all the verses on each subject either but are given as where to find some of these statements in the Bible. Again, what we are trying to accomplish with this is to show you that if we begin at a percentage of less than twenty, and then narrow it down further with the criteria on this list, there will not be billions of people taken in the Rapture.

Of God's true believers, His Word says these things –

- They will confess Jesus Christ as their Lord and Savior to God and to the world – Romans 10:9

- They will believe in their heart God resurrected Jesus from the dead – Romans 10:10

- They will acknowledge their sins and repent – Luke 5:32, 13:3, 2 Corinthians 7:10

- They will believe Jesus' words that He is who He claims to be, the only way to be saved – John 14:6, John 8:24. See also John 17:3, Acts 4:12, Romans 5:1, 1 Timothy 2:5

- They will be born again spiritually, to enter into the kingdom of heaven – John 3:3

- They will surrender their life to Jesus – Matthew 16:24-25, John 12:25-26

- They will do God's will for them as evidence of that surrender. If they have not surrendered their lives to Jesus, He will tell them He doesn't know them – Matthew 7:21-23, Matthew 25:21-45

- They will be fruitful (do good works) for God's kingdom. Good works are evidence they have true saving faith – Matthew 7:16-18, John 15:5, James 2:18, Titus 3:8

Now I want to make sure there is no misunderstanding in what these verses from God's Word are saying in relation to how a person is saved or not. This list appears to be primarily things that are *done* by a true believer, and there should be no misunderstanding how this relates to being *saved* because in the context of this book, being saved would mean being taken in the Rapture.

There is NOTHING we can do to contribute to our being saved. I don't know how to put it any clearer than that. Each one of us can only be saved by God's grace, through faith in what God already did for us in Jesus' life, death and resurrection (Ephesians 2:8-9). Jesus' death on the cross was a necessary payment for the sins of the world for all time, past, present and future, yours and mine (Hebrews 10:12,14). His resurrection allows us to become spiritually alive now (Ephesians 2:1-6), and also physically alive again someday after our death (1 Corinthians 15:42-44), and allows us to have a relationship with God the Father and Jesus both in this life (Hebrews 7:24) and the eternal life to come (Revelation 21:3).

Here's one of the most often pointed to proofs texts from God's Word regarding being saved -

"For by (God's) grace you have been saved, through faith (in Jesus). And this is not your own doing; it is the gift of God, not a result of (good) works, so that no one may boast." – Ephesians 2:8-9, ESV

What that list is, then, is what God's Word says WILL happen in the life of a true believer as evidence they have truly received the gift of God's grace. Received it through a genuine faith, not a fake one, and thus are saved.

If you want more explanation for any or all of the points on our list, you can read about them in the appendix to this chapter. If you feel you know them well enough already and feel like you're ready to make a good guess as to how many might go in the Rapture, let's do that now.

So, we started with less than twenty percent. When we add this partial list of proofs from God's Word that shows a believer has truly accepted Jesus as their Savior, what percent do you think it is now? Fifteen? Ten? Less? Honestly, I think it's less than ten.

If ten percent of the population will be taken in the Rapture, that would currently be about 760 million people. Do you think there are 760 million people in the world that fit into our (partial) list from God's Word so far? Possibly? Let's examine further.

As of September 2018, Wikipedia has a list of all counties in the world and the number of those in each country who claim to be Christians. The total amount at the bottom of the column as of this writing is 2,431,209,718. Well above our number, and 32% of the current population of 7.6 billion. Does that sound like a percentage Jesus was talking about in Matthew 7? He said, "Only a few find it" (the gate to eternal life). How about after adding our (partial) list of from God's Word? An honest answer would be – no. So where are we going wrong here?

Well, that number combines all Roman Catholics, Protestants and any other religious groups that claim they are Christian, but all of those groups don't have the same beliefs. All of them can't be correct when it comes to what God's saving grace is and how it is received. So just by that observation alone, we can reduce that number quite a bit. For a closer look at the differences of many of the groups that call themselves Christians, see the appendix to this chapter at the back of the book. Obviously, the people that don't get taken in the Rapture that were calling themselves Christians were not really Christians after all.

There will be many millions of people that thought they had the truth to go to heaven, but in reality, they did not lay down their pride and surrender themselves to God's plan of saving grace through faith in Jesus alone. They felt like they had to contribute to their being saved, or thought they could contribute, and it ended up costing them a chance to go in the Rapture. However, we don't even need to split that up right now to show the number of people taken won't be even close to that many. Let's break it down by population and an honest assessment of how many you think meet our (partial) list from God's Word, and also taking into consideration what Jesus said in Matthew chapter 7.

Three countries make up about 40% of the world's population – China, India and the United States. The current population of China is almost 1.4 billion, India 1.3 billion and the US about 330 million.

Many surveys show that 70% of the population of the US is said to be Christian. If that is true, how come less than 20% of the US population attend church? Not that attending church will save you, it won't. Remember, we can't do anything to contribute to our being saved, but we are always going to go back to our (partial) list of evidence of things that true believers will do if God's grace has truly saved them.

Now there are many countries where attending church could put one's life in danger so that can't always be done. However, if we can attend church without fear of punishment then doing so regularly would be evidence of us surrendering our lives to Jesus, making it a priority to worship God the Father and Jesus as a group of believers and to learn more about God's Word.

Nevertheless, let's use 20% as our initial number for true Christians in the United States that might be taken in the Rapture, and we will refine it later. For China, it's much more difficult to get the percentage of true Christians because Christianity is suppressed by the government and one cannot openly attend church services, but estimates are anywhere between 100 to 150 million people in China are thought to be Christian. Now I have heard it said, and I believe it, that there are more true Christians in China than there are in the US. If being a Christian in China is going to cost you much more in terms of persecution, prison or worse if you are found out, a person would be much more apt to be a true Christian in China than just a Christian in name only.

No matter what country you are from if you could be imprisoned or killed if you are found with a Bible, wouldn't you expect that person who says he or she is a Christian would be much more apt to have truly accepted Jesus as their Savior? That they would not be one to whom Jesus will say, "Away from me, I never knew you" (Matthew 7:23). That would be a logical conclusion.

For India, the country has a current population of 1.3 billion with seven percent listed as Christian, for a total of about 91 million people. Since it would be harder to be a Christian in India than in the US, but probably not as difficult as in China, let's say 50% are true Christians there. So, now let's start to put some numbers together. In countries where it is very dangerous to be a Christian, we will assume a higher percentage of Christians there (75%) fit into our (partial) list from God's Word and indeed are true believers. For countries where it isn't quite so dangerous to be a Christian, but still, much harder than in the United States, let's start with a ratio of half and adjust it from there.

So, if we start with a generous estimate of twenty percent of the population of the United States will be taken in the Rapture. Add to that 75% of the Christians in China (from the 150 million estimate) and 50% from India (from the 91 million estimate), we get somewhere around 225 million people from the three most populous countries in the world possibly taken in the Rapture. If we add the next seven countries in terms of the highest population using the percentage Wikipedia shows claiming to be Christians and assuming 50% of them fulfill the (partial) list from God's Word, we have a list that looks like this –

Country	Population	Christians	If 50% True Christians
Indonesia	263 million	42 million	21 million
Brazil	209 million	180 million*	90 million*
Pakistan	208 million	2.5 million	1.25 million
Nigeria	204 million	100 million	50 million
Bangladesh	160 million	4 million	2 million
Russia	142 million	95 million**	47.5 million**
Japan	126 million	2 million	1 million

See appendix to this chapter for reasons that number cannot be correct, and thus the second number of people taken in the Rapture cannot be correct either. These reasons also apply to other countries like Mexico or anywhere else where nearly the entire population is counted as Roman Catholic.

**Also see appendix for reasons this number cannot be correct as the Eastern Orthodox Church should also not be considered Biblical Christianity.*

To this point, we have counted almost 60% of the world's population, and we are at about 435 million people. Do you still think there will be possibly 760 million people taken in the Rapture? Still a possibility? Let's look further at God's Word.

We mentioned in our (partial) list from God's Word some of the things that true believers will do as evidence that they have truly accepted Jesus as their only hope for being saved. If you have already read the appendix for more explanation on each of the points on our list, you probably have already answered 'no' for whether you believe there are currently 760 million people on the earth with true saving faith. For those that haven't read the appendix yet, we need to make sure we understand the relationship between saving faith and what that will produce in a person compared to someone who claims to believe in Jesus but shows no outward signs of that faith.

No one can fool God. He knows if we have true faith in Jesus or not. The Bible says God knows the words we speak (Psalm 139:4), our thoughts (Psalm 139:2) and our hearts (Psalm 139:23). God's Word also says there is no place we can go where He can't see us (Jeremiah 23:24). Which means if anyone knew if we have truly accepted Jesus as our Savior and are showing evidence of our being a true believer, God would know.

Jesus told many stories called parables to the people describing what saving faith would look like, and what it would produce in a person. Let's look at one of them. Jesus told this parable to a large crowd that had gathered from many towns to hear him –

"A farmer went out to plant his seed. As he scattered it across his field, some seed fell on a footpath, where it was stepped on, and the birds ate it. Other seed fell among rocks. It began to grow, but the plant soon wilted and died for lack of moisture. Other seed fell among thorns that grew up with it and choked out the tender plants. Still, other seed fell on fertile soil. This seed grew and produced a crop that was a hundred times as much as had been planted!" When he had said this, he called out, "Anyone with ears to hear should listen and understand." – Luke 8:4-8

When His disciples asked him what the parable meant, Jesus replied–

"This is the meaning of the parable: The seed is God's Word. The seeds that fell on the footpath represent those who hear the message, only to have the devil come and take it away from their hearts and prevent them from believing and being saved. The seeds on the rocky soil represent those who hear the message and receive it with joy. But since they don't have deep roots, they believe for a while, then they fall away when they face temptation. The seeds that fell among the thorns represent those who hear the message, but all too quickly the message is crowded out by the cares and riches and pleasures of this life. And so, they never grow into maturity. And the seeds

that fell on the good soil represent honest, good-hearted people who hear God's word, cling to it, and patiently produce a huge harvest." – Luke 8:11-15

What may not be so evident at first glance is that the Word of God must find root in a person's heart. For the Bible says it is with our heart that we truly believe, not our mind (Romans 10:10). Have you ever heard it said or said it yourself, that someone was in your heart or someone has your heart? Your heart is what Jesus wants. If a person hasn't given their heart to Him (meaning Jesus is not in their heart) then how will that person be able to do all the things from our (partial) list from God's Word? The answer is, they won't be able to do them.

We have seen the word 'fruit' a few times in this book, and God's Word says fruit (also known as good works) is what true believers will produce if they are doing the things from that (partial) list. Jesus ends the story by saying people in whose hearts the Word of God takes root and grows will produce a crop 'a hundredfold.' When His disciples asked Him to explain what that meant, Jesus said it means those people will bear much fruit. Bearing fruit is important because it is linked to another word we see Jesus often use in the Bible – repent.

When Jesus was on the earth, He told people everywhere to repent and believe in Him to be saved. The order of those words is important. If He said to believe and repent, one could say repentance is a good thing but is not necessarily required to be saved. However, every time Jesus used the word repent, He said it either by itself (Matthew 4:17, Luke 13:3,5) or repent and believe (Mark 1:15). If Jesus was telling people to repent and be saved, or repent and believe and be saved, we can conclude that repentance is a necessary step in our salvation. It is part of a true saving faith in Jesus Christ.

So what does the word repent, or more specifically it's active form, repentance, mean? Also, how is repentance linked to producing fruit (good works)? Repentance means a changing of the mind or a turning away from something. So in the context of what Jesus is telling a true believer to do when He says to repent, is to change our mind about sin and to turn from our sins. That doesn't mean we won't sin when we have a true saving faith, but rather sin should no longer have the control over our lives that it once had. If we truly have turned from sin and changed our mind about it, then there should be a conscious desire not to sin in our thoughts, words, and deeds.

Another way to put it is when we turn from sin, we acknowledge that we understand –

- How serious God takes sin

- What an abomination sin is to Him

- Why sin deserves eternal punishment

- And why God requires that we turn from sin as part of a true saving faith

When Jesus calls on people to repent, He is asking them to acknowledge their sinfulness before God, which will at the same time make them realize their need for a Savior in Christ Jesus. If you truly believe sin is that bad, you will understand why Jesus had to die on a cross and be raised to life again to pay for your sins. Then you will be much more anxious and appreciative to receive that gift of God's forgiveness for your sins through faith in what Jesus did for you on the cross.

So then, repentance is evidence that a person has a true saving faith in Jesus and is why Jesus often said repent and believe, one after the other…in that order. The progression looks like this –

- A person hears the Word of God and realizes all the things the Bible says about sin are true.

- He or she is a sinner before a holy and just God and without some way of forgiveness they will be condemned and punished severely for their sins.

- Their mind has now been changed about sin and they are now in a state of repentance.

- The next step is belief in God's promise that the only way to eternal life, and to avoid the deserved punishment for their sin, is through faith in what Jesus did for that person in His life, death on the cross, and resurrection from the dead.

If you don't believe you deserve to be punished for your sin, you still have not understood how God views sin, and you are not in a state of repentance. We already discussed how important repentance is for our salvation; one must repent and believe. For when a person repents and believes, Jesus comes to reside in their heart (Ephesians 3:17), through the gift of the Holy Spirit (Galatians 4:6), who was sent by God (John 15:26).

However, it doesn't stop there. The Bible says we can, and should, prove our repentance through the doing of good works; the producing of good fruit (Matthew 3:8, Acts 26:20). Why should we prove our repentance? Because God is going to test our faith to prove it is not dead, for God knows a dead faith cannot save anyone.

In the book of James, we find God's Word telling us that a living faith will produce good works, but a dead faith (that cannot save a person) will not –

"What good is it, dear brothers and sisters, if you say you have faith but don't show it by your actions? Can that kind of faith save anyone? Suppose you see a brother or sister who has no food or clothing, and you say, "Good-bye and have a good day; stay warm and eat well"—but then you don't give that person any food or clothing. What good does that do?" – James 2:14-16

"Now someone may argue, "Some people have faith; others have good deeds." But I say, "How can you show me your faith if you don't have good deeds? I will show you my faith by my good deeds." You say you have faith, for you believe that there is one God. Good for you! Even the demons believe this, and they treble in terror. How foolish! Can't you see that faith without good deeds is useless?" – James 2:18-20

"Just as the body is dead without breath, so also faith is dead without good works." – James 2:26

This is important! Look at what Jesus said on two different occasions about what will happen to those who are not producing good fruit (not doing good works for Him) –

"You can identify them (true believers) by their fruit, that is, by the way they act. Can you pick grapes from thorn bushes, or figs from thistles? A good tree produces good fruit, and a bad tree produces bad fruit. A good tree can't produce bad fruit, and a bad tree can't produce good fruit. So

every tree that does not produce good fruit is chopped down and thrown into the fire. " – Matthew 7:16-19

"I am the true grapevine, and my Father is the gardener. He cuts off every branch of mine (that has a dead faith) that doesn't produce fruit, and he prunes the branches that do bear fruit so they will produce even more. You have already been pruned and purified by the message I have given you. Remain in me (through faith), and I will remain in you (in your heart). For a branch cannot produce fruit if it is severed from the vine, and you cannot be fruitful unless you remain in me. Yes, I am the vine; you are the branches. Those who remain in me, and I in them, will produce much fruit. For apart from me you can do nothing. Anyone who does not remain in me is thrown away like a useless branch and withers. Such branches are gathered into a pile to be burned." – John 15-1-6

In both cases, Jesus said those that do not produce good fruit will be cut down (trees that don't produce good fruit) or cut off (unfruitful branches) and will be thrown into the fire. What is the fire? Hell! Do you see the importance of good works proving a person has a true faith if they claim to be a Christian? We already mentioned how no one could fool God about whether they have a true saving faith and thus would (or would not) be taken in the Rapture. So now let's go back to our percentages again.

What percentage do you think there are of people in the United States that claim to be Christians who are doing good works because they have truly received God's gift of saving grace and have Jesus residing their hearts through the Holy Spirit? Do you still think it could be 20%? Before you answer that, let's clarify what 'good fruit' looks.

There is a passage from God's Word (Galatians 5:22-23) that describes what good fruit will look like. It says in the life of true believer you will be able to see these things acted out in their daily lives – love, joy, peace, patience, kindness, goodness, gentleness, faithfulness and self-control. If 20% of the people in the United States today had saving faith and were practicing all those things, would the country be in the kind of condition it is today?

If 20% of the people were practicing (<u>fill in word from list</u>)

- Love – Would 53% of all marriages in the United States end in divorce? (1)

- Joy – Would 1 in 6 Americans be taking some form of antidepressants and would the percentage of Americans using antidepressants have doubled from 1999 to 2012? (2)

- Peace – Would police officers be killed at one every 58 hours in the United States over the last ten years? (3)

- Patience – Would a person be the slowest car on the freeways when they drive the speed limits? (I can attest to that one)

- Kindness – Would America have the kind of partisan politics where police have to show up in riot gear when two political parties hold a rally in the same location? (4)

- Goodness – Would America have the highest percentage of people in prison in the world? (5)

- Gentleness – Would Grand Theft Auto V be the best-selling video game of all time in the U.S.? More than 85 million copies sold. (6)

- Faithfulness – Would less than 18% of those who call themselves Christians in the U.S. regularly attend church? (7)

- Self-control – Would the United States government and its citizens, combining the federal deficit, home loans, car loans, credit card balances, student loans, and other liabilities be more than 60 trillion dollars in debt? (8)

Now that you have all this information, what do you think now? I hope you would agree with me that if 20% of Americans were doing the things on our (partial) list and producing the kind of good fruit that God's Word describes, we would not be able to cite statistics like these. Just in case there is someone who thinks it is still possible that 20% of Americans will be taken in the Rapture, let's add a list of people who the Bible says will definitely not be going.

According to God's Word, these kinds of people will not inherit the Kingdom of God and thus will not be taken in the Rapture –

- Those who practice fortune telling, sorcery, cast spells or mediums who consult the dead (Deuteronomy 18:10-11)

- Anyone who thinks a man-made image can be their god, anyone who worships created things, which includes the sun, stars, moon or anything in nature (Romans 1:23)

- Gossips and slanderers, God haters, those without love for others, those who are not merciful to others (Romans 1:29)

- Anyone who indulges in fornication, idolatry, adultery, homosexuality, thievery, greed, slander and cheating of others (1 Corinthians 6:9-10)

- Anyone who engages in sexual immorality, debauchery, idolatry, witchcraft, hatred of others, jealousy, envy, fits of rage, selfish ambition, or is a drunkard (Galatians 5:19-20)

- No immoral, impure or greedy person (Ephesians 5:5)

- Anyone who is a lover of themselves, a lover of money, who is boastful or proud, abusive to others, disobedient to their parents, ungrateful to God, unforgiving of others, has no self-control, does not love good, is treacherous, rash, conceited, a lover of pleasure (2 Timothy 2:3)

- Those who do not care for their immediate family members (1 Timothy 5:8)

- Those who want to get rich (1 Timothy 6:9)

- Those who claim to know God but deny Him by doing evil (Titus 1:16)

- Those who cannot control their tongue/swearing (James 1:26)

- Anyone who loves the world (James 4:4, 1 John 2:15)

- Those who are vile, unbelieving, murderers, those who practice magic, put anything before God (idolaters) and all liars (Revelation 21:8)

So I ask one last time, what percentage do you think will go in the Rapture now? Less than 20, less than 15, less than 10? I believe everything that is revealed in God's Word indicates it will be less than 10. So when we apply our (partial) list to the other countries around the world, what percentages should we use for them? I don't think we can pick an exact number, but the whole idea is, after carefully examining God's Word, do you think there could be 760 million people in the world taken in the Rapture? Not likely, not 760 million adults anyway.

How could the age of a person factor into that?

I've been waiting to add one last thing to our equation, and if it's true (and God's Word seems to indicate that it is), this will bring us up to that number and way past it. That last thing is this – it appears that all children under a certain age of accountability will be taken too. How can we know this? Well, God's Word doesn't say it outright, but there are several clues that God has revealed that lead to that conclusion.

Let's go over them in the next chapter because having all children under a certain age disappear in the blink of an eye? That is something that should be covered in depth as the effects this will have on those left behind, especially on unbelievers who have their children taken away from them, will be absolutely horrendous.

4

Children Taken in the Rapture

The first clue we have regarding an age of accountability in the Bible comes from the story of God leading His people out of slavery in Egypt. God did ten miraculous signs (plagues) to prove to Pharaoh, and also to God's chosen people Israel, that He is God and there is no other (Exodus chapters 7-11). These miracles were not only witnessed by Pharaoh and the people of Egypt, but they were also seen by the Israelites.

After the ten plagues, Pharaoh let the Israelites go but later changed his mind and sent his army after them. When all hope seemed lost, God provided a means for them to escape by parting the Red Sea so they could walk through it. When the Egyptian army followed into the space God had opened up in the sea, God caused the waters to come together again and destroyed them all (Exodus chapter 14).

Two years later the Israelites came to a land that God said He would give to them, but they had to conquer the people already living there. They sent 12 men to spy out the land for 40 days, and when they came back, ten of the men said Israel could not conquer the land while only Caleb and Joshua had faith they could do it (see Numbers 13). The ten men convinced all the adults of Israel except four, Moses, Aaron, Joshua and Caleb, that they could not defeat the inhabitants of the land God was giving them. So God said this –

"As surely as I live, and as surely as the earth is filled with the glory of the Lord, not one of these people (who have rejected my offer of a promised land) will ever enter that land. They have all seen my glorious presence and the miraculous signs I performed both in Egypt and in the wilderness (including the parting of the Red Sea), but again and again they have tested me by refusing to listen to my voice." – Numbers 14:21-22

As a result of that decree, God punished all the adults, but *not* the children –

"In the wilderness your bodies will fall – every one of you twenty years or more who was counted in the census and who has grumbled against me.

Not one of you will enter the land except Caleb and Joshua, As for your children...I will bring them in to enjoy the land you have rejected." – Numbers 14:29-31, NIV

Since it took two years until they got to the promised land (Numbers 10:11), God was not considering anyone under eighteen years of age (when He brought them out of Egypt) to be guilty of rejecting Him. Since we know God doesn't change (Malachi 3:6) and people were eternally saved the same way then, dying in faith, that they are now (Hebrews 11:13), couldn't we use these facts to help determine if children will be taken in the Rapture?

Does this mean we can count all children under the age of eighteen as going in the Rapture? Well, not necessarily. The fact that God did not count them as rejecting him then doesn't mean they couldn't still reject him later. It just meant they were not condemned to die in the wilderness at that time because God did not consider them old enough to make that kind of decision that would have eternal consequences. But it's a good start at trying to establish when God considers someone old enough to reject Him, and punishing them eternally if they die in that condition.

The second clue we have that there is an age of accountability is because of what King David said about the death of his newborn baby. David said he shall someday go to him, but his baby that died would not return to him. (2 Samuel 12:23)

David was called a man after God's own heart (Acts 13:22), and God said He would raise David from the dead in the future to rule over Israel again (Jeremiah 30:9). So do you think David is in heaven right now or in hell? Do you think God would have allowed David's words regarding his son dying and going to heaven to be written in the Bible if it wasn't true? Of course not.

So what's going on here? We have two examples where we are shown it seems there is some kind of age of accountability for either choosing God or rejecting Him. One was a group where everyone was under the age of eighteen, and the other was a newborn baby. They all would still need God's grace to be saved because the Bible says we are born with a sinful nature that is passed on to us from Adam (Romans 5:12) and that we are even sinful from the womb (Psalm 51:5). One sin is enough to keep us out of heaven because breaking just one of God's laws means we are guilty of breaking them all (James 2:10). So how could a newborn baby who cannot even reason to know who Jesus is, let alone believe in Him as his Savior, be saved?

Well, the answer may come from a few things Jesus said in God's Word. Let's take a look at some examples where Jesus said things that either must be done or not done (in the case of unbelief) to be saved.

"Unless you believe that I am who I claim to be, you will die in your sins." – John 8:24

"Every sin and blasphemy can be forgiven, except blasphemy against the Holy Spirit, which will never be forgiven. Anyone who speaks against the Son of Man (Jesus) can be forgiven, but anyone who speaks against the Holy Spirit will never be forgiven, either in this world or the world to come." – Matthew 12:31-32

"If you declare with your mouth, 'Jesus is Lord,' and believe in your heart that God raised Him from the dead, you will be saved." – Romans 10:9, NIV

Would God condemn a newborn baby who has died to hell because he or she cannot do these things, to accept or reject Jesus? We already saw in the example of David and his newborn baby who died that God does not.

Could a one-year-old, two-year-old, or three-year-old accept or reject Jesus? No.

How about a child four, five or six? Not likely.

Could a child of seven, eight or nine accept or reject Jesus and really understand what they were doing? Doubtful.

How about a child age ten, eleven or twelve? Maybe.

However, would a child even eleven or twelve really understand enough about these things where God would hold them eternally accountable for their decisions? Based on the example of God only holding those who were 18 years or older accountable when the people rejected the Lord after He led them out of Egypt (Jude 5), it appears He would not.

So what can children do that we see in God's Word that indicates they would be taken in the Rapture? They can be children.

"I tell you the truth, unless your turn from your sins and become like little children, you will never get into the kingdom of heaven." – Matthew 18:3

"Then they brought little children to Him, that he might touch them; but the disciples rebuked those who brought them. But when Jesus saw it, He

was greatly displeased and said to them, 'Let the little children come to Me, and do not forbid them; for of such is the kingdom of God.' – Mark 10:13-14, NKJV

"Beware that you do not look down on any of these little ones (children). For I tell you that in heaven their angels are always in the presence of my heavenly Father." – Matthew 18:10

"Are not all angels ministering spirits sent to serve those who will inherit salvation? – Hebrews 1:14, NIV

Doesn't it appear God's saving grace somehow covers a child's sins until God decides they are capable of truly believing (or not believing) those things Jesus said that carry with them eternal consequences?

To believe Jesus is who He claims to be (or not to believe)?

To choose whether to accept the Holy Spirit (or to reject Him)?

To declare with their mouth that Jesus is Lord (or choose not to say it)?

To truly believe in their heart that God raised Jesus from the dead (or not believe it)?

Again, Jesus said unless you become as little children you will by no means enter the kingdom of heaven and of such (children) is the kingdom of God. He also said every child has an angel assigned to them, and then the Bible says angels are only sent to serve those who will inherit salvation? Seems to me like Jesus is saying children are saved up until the point where they knowingly accept or reject Him.

God's Word says Jesus is the same yesterday, today and forever (Hebrews 13:8). So considering all these truths from God's Word, don't you think millions and millions of children would be taken in the Rapture two thousand years later? I think so. But up to what age will they be taken? Can we assume the age of eighteen?

Perhaps we should look again at the example where God allowed all children under the age of eighteen to have the opportunity to survive in the wilderness and return to the land that He promised to give them. It wasn't because everyone under eighteen believed God while their parents did not. I'm sure plenty of them were afraid to go into the land where God was telling them to go. There were giants there! (Numbers 13:28,33). But then we could also ask, why were they afraid to go into the land? They saw the plagues God brought on Egypt, the same as their parents did. They walked through the Red Sea that God parted for them, same as their parents did (Exodus 14:21-22).

So why did God hold all those over eighteen accountable for their unbelief in His ability to give them the land, but for those under eighteen He did not hold them accountable? We can only speculate, but it probably has to do with God deciding that up to a certain point in a person's life, they are too young to fully understand a decision they must make – to have faith in the one true God and faith in His means of grace, or to reject Him.

God makes it clear through the words of Jesus, those are the only two choices a person has –

"Anyone who isn't with me opposes me, and anyone who isn't working with me is actually working against me." – Matthew 12:30

This verse is right before the one we read where Jesus said rejecting the Holy Spirit means that person will not be forgiven. Why is that? Because rejecting the Holy Spirit means rejecting Jesus. There are a few very important words that connect those two verses to indicate rejecting the Holy Spirit means rejecting Jesus.

"Anyone who isn't with me opposes me, and anyone who isn't working with me is actually working against me. So I tell you, every sin and blasphemy can be forgiven, except blasphemy against the Holy Spirit, which will never be forgiven." – Matt 12:30-31 (emphasis mine)

So, to all the Israelites under the age of eighteen that came out of Egypt, it appears God could have put it this way, 'Even though you saw my mighty works in delivering you from Egypt, you are too young to understand that rejecting me at this time will have eternal consequences, so I won't hold you accountable…yet.'

That is the key - not yet. Not until they reach a certain point where God would hold them accountable. It is quite possible (and most likely) that many of those that God led back into the wilderness that were under the age of eighteen eventually rejected Him too and they did not survive to see the promised land either. However, the important point to consider is that God gave them more time to choose to have faith in Him or not. This is why we cannot assume every child under the age of eighteen will be taken in the Rapture because there will still be time after the Rapture to come to saving faith in Jesus or to reject Him.

From the time God begins pouring out His wrath on the world during the Tribulation until Jesus comes back to set foot on the earth again, the Bible says there will be seven years (Daniel 9:25-27). God may want anyone who would reach their own age of accountability by the end of those seven years to stay on the earth and either choose Him (through faith in Jesus) or reject Him. There is no way to know for sure, but we cannot assume all children under the age of eighteen will be taken in the Rapture. The number is too arbitrary, and a just God would not operate that way.

If a person who is seventeen and does not believe in Jesus as His Savior is taken in the Rapture, and another person who is eighteen and doesn't believe either is not taken simply because he is one year older than the other, where is the justice in that? We are told numerous times in the Bible that God is just (Psalm 9:16, 45:6, 50:6, 89:14, 101:1, 111:7, Isaiah 30:18, 45:21, 61:18, 2 Thessalonians 1:6, 1 Peter 2:23, Revelation 16:5) and that would not be just. Now taking all children that would not make it to the age of eighteen by the end of those seven years? That is something that could most certainly happen based on the example we saw where God did not consider anyone under eighteen being guilty of rejecting Him when He brought those children out of Egypt.

Would taking all children up to 11 or 12 seem like a better age where one would believe a just God would not hold them accountable for making a decision that has eternal consequences? It does to me, probably to most of us. Honestly, I don't think we can assume a certain age though because God's Word says one-quarter of the earth's population will die before the end of the third year following the Rapture (Revelation 6:8). By the end of the fifth year, one half the earth's population will die (Rev 9:18), and if it lasted longer than seven years no one would remain alive (Matthew 24:22).

God knows the individual ages at which all of us will die (Psalm 139:16), so He most certainly knows who will make it to their age of accountability during the Tribulation and who will not. Based on the example we saw of Him not holding those who came out of Egypt under the age of eighteen accountable for their unbelief, and knowing God does not change (Malachi 3:6), and that Jesus does not change (Hebrews 13:8). It would seem like all children that God knows will not reach their own age of accountability seven years after the Rapture, that they would be taken. That would mean all children under the age of 12 will probably be taken, as well as all those that will not reach their own age of accountability within the next 1 to 7 years after the Rapture.

So now that we have a better idea of those who will be taken in the Rapture, both adults and children, what is our best guess as to how many will be taken? How many children are there under the age of eighteen in the world? Estimates vary, probably because so many countries can't keep accurate records, but there are probably at least two billion children under the age of 18 in the world. How many children are there under the age of 12 in the world? That information is harder to find but if we go by the percentage of children under 12 in the United States (which is about two-thirds of all children under 18) that should get us close.

The current population of the world as of the writing this sentence is 7,661,195,390. Only God knows what the world's population will be at the time of the Rapture, and how many of those will be children that would not make it to age eighteen. If the Rapture happened right now, it would appear those that would be taken would be –

- Anywhere from 600 to 700 million adults (based on our less than 10% model)

- At least 1.3 billion children under the age of 12

- Any of the other 600+ million children that God knew would not reach their age of accountability over the next seven years (probably well over half of them)

- And all babies in the womb! God considers them children before they are born, not after! (Luke 1:41-44). Can you even try to imagine the terrible effects this will have on all pregnant mothers who are not taken at the same time with their babies?

Can you see why the Rapture will be the event that shakes the world to its core?

Now let's turn to what this will all mean (and do) to the world after the Rapture has occurred. Let's begin by talking about a world without children and how that might look.

I would like to begin by saying –

It is my sincere hope and prayer for those reading this that if you are not currently saved through faith in Jesus alone, and you have children, that you do not think anything bad will have happened to your children if they one day disappear along with over a billion other children all over the world. In fact, it will be just the opposite. Your children will think something terrible has happened to you because you are not with them, and they will be correct.

Anyone not taken in the Rapture will be living in a world that has no children under the age of 11 or 12, none that will be born within the next ten months, and possibly not that many teenage children either. Can one even imagine what the ramifications will be? There is no way to cover it all or even to imagine it all, but let's consider a few things.

First and foremost, everyone who had a child or children taken in the Rapture will fall into a state of despair that will make it hard to function anymore. I suspect there will be tens of thousands or possibly hundreds of thousands of parents who may commit suicide when they realize what has happened. They have lost their children and believe they will never see them again. Of course, that is not true. They *can* see them again if they receive the gift of grace still available to them through faith in Jesus, but there will be many that will not understand that and take their own lives.

My prayer is that God will show as many people as possible, both before the Rapture and after, that those who might commit suicide either out of despair or a desire to try to be with their children again, that they would come to know there is only one way to see them. By receiving God's forgiveness of their sins, through faith in Jesus, as their only hope of salvation. I pray they would use the time they have left to tell others to do the same. God is always directing people who are not saved to His Son Jesus, and the Rapture is something that He will use to do that on a massive scale.

It would be better for a person to lose their kids for a time at the Rapture if it results in their salvation later than to die in a state of rejecting Jesus and have no chance of ever being with them again. The Rapture will be something that God will use to end up saving millions of people that may have died rejecting Jesus otherwise (Revelation 7:9-14) whether it is a parent whose kids were taken and they were not or anyone else who wasn't taken. Many people will see, by way of the Rapture, that God keeps His promises and that will lead them to believe in His greatest promise – the forgiveness of their sins and eternal life through faith in Jesus Christ.

Better to be saved after the Rapture than not at all. However, because they missed the Rapture of all true believers, they will have to live in a completely changed world. A world that has had most of its children taken out of it. What will that world look like and what will happen as a result?

I don't think the anguish of billions of parents over the entire world whose children were taken, but they were not, can be put into words. When one parent loses a child, it's hard to imagine what they are going through. How can anyone possibly imagine that on a global scale, billions of parents losing their children all at one time? This will be one of the significant factors, in addition to losing almost a tenth of the world's workforce, that will lead to a complete and total economic collapse after the Rapture. We will discuss the economic collapse in more detail in the last chapter of the book, but we can be sure all these things and more will happen once all children under 12 years of age, along with many older children, are removed from the world all at the same time —

- Tens of thousands of suicides of parents who lost their kids, including many pregnant mothers who had babies taken from their wombs

- No babies will be born for the next ten months

- Any company that relies on children as their target market will be out of business instantly

- All preschools, kindergartens and grade schools will close immediately and without any incoming students, all high schools will close within a few years putting millions of teachers out of work all over the world

There is no way to know everything that will happen as a result of the world having most of its children taken all at the same time, but isn't this already enough to not want to be left here after it occurs? We haven't even discussed the extensiveness of the economic collapse that will lead to mass starvation and global war as God pours out His wrath on an unbelieving world. Do you think you can afford to wait to repent of your sins if you haven't done that yet? The Rapture could happen soon (discussed in the next chapter).

Don't delay! Confess your sins before God and receive the gift of His saving grace through faith in Jesus' death on the cross and resurrection from the dead. God did for us what we could not do for ourselves. He became the perfect sacrifice for sin that was required in Jesus Christ (Hebrews 9:14). God in the flesh (Hebrews 2:14), one sacrifice for all time (Hebrews 7:27), for all people (Romans 3:25-26). Since the death of Christ, for those who would confess with their mouth that Jesus is Lord and believe in their heart that God raised Him from the dead, they will be saved (Romans 10:9). In repentance ask for God's forgiveness through the blood of Jesus (Hebrews 10:19) that was shed on the cross and His resurrection (1 Corinthians 15:13-17). Ask Him to send His Holy Spirit into your heart. God's Word promises He will not reject you for anything you have done (John 6:37).

5

Unfulfilled Prophecy
and
Timing of the Rapture

I struggled with whether to include this chapter and maybe not even mention unfulfilled prophecies that may or may not have to happen before the Rapture takes place. I wasn't sure if I wanted to include it because prophecy is something that can be confusing at times, and many avoid it like the plague. Many will not read the book of Revelation because it is mainly prophetic in nature. However, ultimately, this chapter needed to be included for a few reasons.

First, and most importantly, it needed to be included because this chapter will explain the title of the book. Without it, the book would have to have a different name. Second, the way the book is written it is not necessary to completely understand these prophecies and still get all the information I wanted to pass on from God's Word about the Rapture and what will happen after it occurs.

The third reason why I decided to include it is that I think it lends credibility to the book. It shows how thoroughly I have studied the subject of the Rapture, including the timing of the Rapture. Many people are interested in the timing, and there have been entire books written about the timing of the Rapture. We don't have the space to go into such a thorough explanation here. However, there are two prophecies in the Bible that have not been fulfilled yet, and many say one or both of them must take place before the Rapture can occur. Let's take a look at those prophecies, see how they go together, and see if it appears that they must happen before the Rapture.

The first prophecy is a war that will occur between Israel and groups of people from several nations that will unite to try to destroy them. It is called the Psalm 83 war because it is all laid out in Psalm 83. These nations and groups of people conspire to try to wipe Israel off the map so that Israel's name will be 'remembered no more.' (Psalm 83:4)

These nations and peoples will form an alliance and go to war with Israel (Psalm 83:6-8)

- Tents of Edom (Palestinians)

- Ishmaelites (Saudi Arabia)

- Moab (Central and Southern Jordan)

- Gebal (Nothern Lebanon)

- Ammon (Northern Jordan)

- Amalek (Arabs living in the Sinai Peninsula)

- Philistia (Hamas)

- Tyre (Southern Lebanon and Hezbollah)

- Assyria (Syria and Northern Iraq)

However, Israel will win the war decisively (Ps 83:13-16), and these groups will cease to exist as countries and as organized peoples (verse 17). Then most of Israel's land will be restored to them that God promised to Abraham, the father of the nation of Israel. The boundaries of Israel (that have never changed) are described in places like Genesis 15:18, Exodus 23:31 and Deuteronomy 11:24 in the Bible. Now, this war hasn't happened yet as Israel is currently about the size of New Jersey, and Jordan and Lebanon are not considered part of Israel.

Now there is nothing in the prophecy that indicates this must happen before the Rapture. However, this event does have to happen before another attempted invasion of Israel prophesied in Ezekiel 38-39 can take place, and many say (with good arguments) that the invasion spoken of in Ezekiel has to happen before the Rapture can occur. Let's take a look at that prophecy, how it ties into the Psalm 83 war, and see if it has to happen before the Rapture.

It says several nations will attack Israel at the same time from the North, South, and East. These nations will attack Israel at the same time (Ezekiel:38-3-6) –

- Magog/Rosh (Russia and nations to the south like Ukraine and Kazakhstan)

- Meshech (Western Turkey)

- Tubal (Eastern Turkey)

- Persia (Iran)

- Cush (Sudan and Ethiopia)

- Put (Libya and Algeria)

- Gomer (Northern Turkey)

- Beth-Togarmah (Southern Turkey)

There may be other nations currently living now in those territories from when the prophecy Ezekiel was written, but even if it is just these nations, Israel will be attacked from three sides at once. They will do this to try to take 'great plunder' from Israel (Ezekiel 38:12-13). God, Himself will defeat them by sending torrential rains (floods), hailstones, and fire and brimstone from the sky (verse 22). He will do this to show His enemies, Israel, and the whole world that He is the Lord (Ezekiel 38:19, 23, 39:7).

Now obviously this hasn't happened yet either. However, why does the Psalm 83 war have to occur before the prophecy spoken of in Ezekiel 38-39 can happen? Well, there are a few things from the prophecy in Ezekiel regarding Israel that haven't been put in place yet – but would be satisfied after Israel's victory in the Psalm 83 war.

First, the prophecy says these nations attack Israel when they are dwelling safely in a land without walls (Ezekiel 38:11). Could Israel ever dwell safely in their land without using walls if they didn't first defeat all those groups of people listed in Psalm 83? Could Israel ever take down the West Bank defense wall unless they first defeat the groups listed in Psalm 83? That wall must be gone before the prophecy in Ezekiel can take place. After Israel wins the Psalm 83 war, that wall won't be needed anymore and can be taken down.

One other thing mentioned in Ezekiel 39 says Israel will need seven months to bury all the dead soldiers that God will destroy, and the place that the bodies will be buried is said to be *within* the land of Israel (Ezekiel 39:11-

12). However, that place where God's Word says Israel will bury the bodies is in current day Jordan to the east of the Dead Sea. After Israel wins the Psalm 83 war, the country of Jordan will be Israel's territory again. It seems evident to me, and hopefully to you too, that the Psalm 83 war must take place before the invasion spoken of in Ezekiel 38-39 can occur.

There are other reasons the Psalm 83 war must take place first as well, such as the building of the third Jewish temple. A third Jewish temple is spoken of in many places in God's Word, so it *will* be built. However, the groups of people listed in Psalm 83 would never allow it to be built on the current site of the Dome of the Rock, which is the only place Israel will ever consider building a third temple. So those nations and groups of people must first be defeated before it can happen. However, an explanation of all that, and other things is not needed (and not desired on my part) as it takes us further away from the main focus of this book which is the Rapture and its after-effects on the world.

We do need to conclude though the question of – How do these two prophecies fit into the timing of the Rapture, and do they need to occur before it happens? There are a couple of things to consider here. First, the Rapture will happen sometime before the seven-year Tribulation where God will pour out His wrath on an unbelieving world. We discussed in the chapter about the Rapture itself why true believers won't be on earth when that happens (because they are not appointed to God's wrath) so we won't go over that again. However, here is where we need to take into consideration some timing of the events given in the prophecy from Ezekiel.

First, if the Rapture occurs and the Psalm 83 war hasn't happened yet, there doesn't seem to be enough time for that war plus everything else written about in Ezekiel 38 and 39 to take place within the next seven years. There will need to be time between the Psalm 83 war and the invasion of Ezekiel for Israel to build up its wealth to the point where the other nations would want to take it. Also, there would need to be time to take down the walls. In addition, when you add the prophecy from Ezekiel 39, which says Israel will take seven years to dispose of all the weapons that were taken from the millions of dead soldiers that God destroyed (Ezekiel 39:9-10), the math doesn't work.

Second, even if the Psalm 83 war had already taken place, Israel had built immense wealth, taken down any walls and was living in peace, we know that halfway through the Tribulation the people of Israel will have to flee for their lives from the Antichrist and hide in the mountains that are currently part of southern Jordan. Revelation chapter 12 describes this through the imagery of a woman (Israel) and a dragon (the devil) and how the woman flees for 1260 days (three and a half years) in the wilderness. This would mean Israel could not dispose of the weapons for more than about three and a half years (the first half of Tribulation) if the invasion of Ezekiel took place right after the Rapture. So how do we reconcile all this to be able to say the Rapture could happen before these events take place, rather than after it? Well, there are a couple of ways to do this.

First, God's Word doesn't say those are seven *consecutive* years where Israel will be disposing of the weapons. There could be a break in there where they flee for their lives, temporarily halting the disposing of the weapons, then continue again after Jesus comes back and sets up His thousand-year reign on earth (Rev 20:4). That is a possibility that would allow the Rapture to occur before the invasion of Ezekiel 38-39 takes place.

Ok, that's fine. However, what about the Psalm 83 war and does that have to take place before the Rapture? Israel still would need time after that war to increase their wealth and to take down any walls. So it seems like there should be at least a year or two between those two prophecies. Well, another way, and this seems more likely to me is the Rapture may be the event that sets up the conditions for the Psalm 83 war to take place, followed a year or two later by the invasion from Ezekiel 38-39. When you consider everything that will happen after the Rapture has taken place, one could see how this could happen.

I know you haven't read what happens after the Rapture yet, but the Rapture will devastate the United States (and the world) to such a degree that the groups of people listed in Psalm 83 could be emboldened to attack Israel. The U.S. military will be crippled as a higher percentage of the military will be taken in the Rapture than the civilian population (discussed in the next chapter). If the United States cannot help Israel because of that, it may be the deciding factor in those groups that wanted to attack long ago but did not for fear the U.S. would come to Israel's aid. Israel will still win, and this would set up the conditions for the invasion a year or two later from the prophecy in Ezekiel 38-39. This certainly could happen.

However, what if those seven years Israel needs to dispose of the weapons from the invasion of Ezekiel are consecutive? If they are consecutive, then the Rapture would have to occur at least four or five years before the Tribulation starts. In order for both the Psalm 83 war and the invasion of Ezekiel to take place before Israel will flee to the mountains. This timeline is highly unlikely, however, because God is using the church to bring the message of salvation to the world (2 Corinthians 5:18-20) so why would He remove the church at least four years before the Tribulation starts?

Are you beginning to see why I was hesitant even to mention prophecy in the first place? It can be very confusing. Let me just cut to the chase and tell you what all my years of research and studying of God's Word leads me to believe will possibly happen. I believe –

- Since God created everything in six days and rested on the seventh (Genesis 2:2-3)

- And the apostle Peter, when talking about the end times in 2 Peter chapter 3, said a day to God is like a thousand years and a thousand years like a day (verse 8)

- Since God's perfect number for purification is seven (Psalm 12:6)

- And the number of Satan is 6 (Revelation 13:18)

- And if the last generation Jesus was referring to in Matthew 24:34 was 80 years in length, it would end 6000 years after sin entered the world (Genesis 3)

I believe it is very likely that God has ordained 6000 years for this sinful, fallen earth. At that time, Jesus will come back and remove Satan who is called the god of this age and this world (2 Corinthians 4:4) and set up the millennium where He rules the earth for 1000 years. During that period of time God the Father will rest for 'a day,' and then after a total of 7000 years has been completed, make everything new again like He said He would (Revelation 21:5).

I told you God's perfect number for purification is seven, and gave you the example of God's perfectly pure Word being compared to silver and gold purified seven times in a fire. Why would God choose seven times if seven was not His perfect number for purification? There are so many examples of the number seven being God's number in the Bible that we couldn't cover even a fraction of them in this chapter. However, we can be sure, it's His number. So how about an example of the number seven with regards to sin since I believe God could permanently remove sin from the world after 7000 years. An example where God uses the number seven with regards to the cleansing of sin.

In 2 Kings 5:10 the prophet Elisha told Naaman, who had leprosy, to wash in the Jordan river seven times and then he would be cleansed from his leprosy. Leprosy is a metaphor for sin in the Bible (Leviticus 13:45) and the people at that time also believed those with leprosy *were* being punished for their sin (Numbers 12:9-11). So if Naaman had to wash seven times to be cleansed of his 'sin,' this fits into 7000 years for a sinful earth – 6000 years and Jesus comes back, 1000 years where Jesus reigns on earth, and at the end of 7000 years, God removes sin permanently from the world at that time.

If this is true, that there will be 6000 years from the beginning of time before Jesus returns, then we need to put together a timeline to figure out where we are because that is something we need to know. Guess what, we can do it using the Bible. Here are some timelines to put this all together, and I will list some more references in the back of the book for those that may want even more details.

All the ages of the first ten patriarchs are given in Genesis chapter 5; dates of birth, when the next patriarch was born, and when they died. From this information, we can determine how long it was from when God made Adam until the worldwide flood. The chart looks like this —

Patriarch	Year of Birth	Age when son born	Year of Death
Adam	1	130	930
Seth	130	105	1042
Enosh	235	90	1140
Cainan	325	70	1140
Mahalalel	395	65	1290
Jared	460	162	1422
Enoch	622	65	987 (raptured)
Methuselah	687	187	1656
Lamech	874	182	1651
Noah	1056	500	2006

God's Word says Noah was 600 years old when the flood came (Genesis 7:6) so we know the flood occurred approximately 1656 years after God created Adam. We say approximately because it's unknown whether the fathers had just turned the age listed on the chart when their son was born, or their birthday was coming up soon. That gives us a possible ten-year swing either way. Plus 10 if all the patriarchs had just turned the age listed in the chart as that whole year would still have to take place, and minus 10 if all of them were very close to being one year older, as the year shown only had a few days left in it. Taking the average of five had just turned the age listed in the chart and five would be having another birthday soon gives us a very close estimate of 1656 years from the time God created Adam until He destroyed the world with a flood.

The next timeline to figure out is from after the flood until God gave Abraham the promise that He would make him into a great nation. Genesis chapters 11 and 12 lay this all out. I'm not going to put this into a chart, but it says there were nine generations from Shem (a son of Noah) until Abraham. Shem was 98 years old when the flood was over and had his first son two years later. Adding up the years of those nine generations given in Genesis 11 we get 350 years from Shem's first son until Abraham was born. We add two since Shem's first son was born two years after the flood, plus 75 because the Bible says Abraham was 75 years old when God gave him the promise (Genesis 12:4). Now we are at 2083, (1656+352+75).

We could move that up or down nine years for the same reason as before; nine generations listed without knowing whether the father just had a birthday or would have a birthday soon after the next son was born. However, again, taking half had just turned the age listed in the Bible, and the other four were going to be one year older soon keeps us right about the same 2083, so let's leave it as is.

God's Word says there were 430 years from the time Abraham received the promise until the Exodus from Egypt (Galatians 3:17) and there were 480 years from the Exodus until Solomon started to build the temple (1 Kings 6:1). Now we are up to 2993, (2083+430+480).

So now all we need to know is what year was it on our calendar when Solomon started to build the temple? 1 Kings 6:1 says it was in the fourth year of Solomon's reign that he began to build the temple and most secular writings date his reign from 970 to 931BC. So if Solomon started construction of the temple in 967BC, we add 967 to 2993, and now we are at 3960, which takes us up to 1 AD.

Now we can finish the timeline of the Old Testament if we can determine what year it was that Jesus was crucified as the Bible says The Old Testament (and the old covenant) ended when Jesus died (Hebrews 9). A New Testament (and new covenant) is only in effect after the death of the testator, which God's Word says was Jesus (Hebrews 9:15-17). This means that after Jesus died, the New Testament began.

We can be reasonably certain that Jesus was crucified in 30AD. Follow me on this timeline from Jesus' birth to His death. –

-   We know John the Baptist started his ministry in the 15th year of the reign of Tiberius Caesar (Luke 3:1), which Luke would have considered to be from October 27AD to October 28AD. (1) It was also during that period of time Jesus started His ministry when He came to John to be baptized (Matthew 3:13)

-   The Bible says Jesus was thirty years old when He was baptized (Luke 3:23) and announced Himself as the Messiah (Luke 4:16-21). For Jesus to be thirty years old when He was baptized in 27AD, He had to be born in 5BC (went from 1BC to 1AD, no zero year). This would make Jesus 30 years old at the end of 26AD.

- The book of John records Jesus observing three Passovers during His ministry - John 2:23, 6:4, and 11:55 - being killed on the third one. So Jesus died in the year 30AD.

God's Word says Jesus was crucified during the Passover (John 18:39), and it also says that day was a day of Preparation for the Sabbath day after that (John 19:31). Most people think this means Jesus was crucified on a Friday because the Sabbath day was always on Saturday. However, Jesus could not have been crucified on a Friday and then fulfill the prophecy He said about Himself - That after He was killed He would be in the heart of the earth (hell) for three days and three nights (Matthew 12:40). The only way that Jesus could be in hell for three *nights* before rising again from the dead on a Sunday (John 20:1) would be if He was crucified on a Thursday. Well, guess what?

Records show the Passover date in 30AD was *Thursday*, April 6th. In fact, of all the Passover dates from 26 to 34 AD, the only one that was on a Thursday was in 30AD (2). The reference in John chapter 19 about the day after Jesus' death being a Sabbath day is talking about the first day after Passover being the first day of the Feast of Unleavened Bread; which is *always* the first day after Passover, and it is *always* a Sabbath day no matter what day it falls on during the week (Leviticus 23:5-7). Thus, any reference in the Bible to the day after Jesus was crucified as being a Sabbath day is talking about a Friday, and *not* a Saturday.

This all fits perfectly regarding what God's Word reveals about the year Jesus was born and the year He died. It is because of all these proofs from God's Word, which are confirmed by the only Passover occurring on a Thursday over a span of nine years being in 30AD, we can be reasonably certain Jesus died in 30AD.

So now we take 3960 years, plus 30 years until Jesus died and we get 3990. We also have to add in the seven years from the prophecy in Daniel 9, as those are Old Testament years that haven't taken place yet. Now we are at approximately 3997 years for the Old Testament. Again, we say approximately because there were 19 generations used in our chronology that could move that number of 3997 up or down by 19 years. This is speculation on my part, but I believe God would use a round number for Old Testament years, and I could see 4000 as a number He would use. I believe that because 40 is a number that God uses a lot in the Bible and 4000 would be a natural extension of it.

Here are some of the examples of God using the number 40 in the Bible–

- God sent rain on the earth for 40 days and 40 nights when He destroyed the earth in a flood (Genesis 7:12)

- God appeared in the burning bush to Moses after he hid for 40 years in the land of Midian (Acts 7:30)

- God exiled the Israelites for 40 years in the desert when they disobeyed his command to conquer the land that He promised to give them (Numbers 14:33)

- Moses was on Mount Sinai for 40 days and 40 nights receiving the Ten Commandments from God (Deuteronomy 9:11)

- God allowed King David to reign 40 years in Israel (2 Samuel 5:4)

- God allowed King Solomon to reign 40 years in Israel (1 Kings 11:42)

- The prophet Jonah told the city of Nineveh in 40 days God would overthrow it if the people did not repent (Jonah 3:4)

- Jesus was tempted for 40 days by Satan (Luke 4:2)

- Jesus remained on earth 40 days after His resurrection (Acts 1:3)

Considering God used the number 40 in these examples, and many others, it just seems more likely to me that He would not ordain such an odd number of 3997 years for the Old Testament when that is so close to 4000.

So, considering we are at about 4000 years for the Old Testament, if God has ordained 6000 years for this earth before Jesus comes back at the Rapture, then that would mean the New Testament would last about 2000 years. If Jesus was crucified in 30AD that would mean those 2000 years would be over in 2030. This would mean the Rapture would have to occur sometime before the year 2030. When we combine this with the fact that the year 2028 would be eighty years since Israel became a nation again, and 2028 is approximately 6000 years from the time God created the world, I believe it is very likely eighty years was the amount of time Jesus was referring to when He said the last generation would not pass away before He returns again.

If the seven years spoken of in Ezekiel 39 where Israel will be disposing of the weapons from the countries who attacked them are consecutive, that would mean the Rapture would have to occur very soon. If they are not consecutive, that would mean the Rapture could happen closer to 2028 - 2030, because as we already said, why would God take the church out of the world four years before He had to when He is using it to save souls?

It is my opinion that the seven years are not consecutive, but will be broken up when the Israelites have to flee for their lives, and continued again into the millennium when Jesus is ruling on earth. That would mean the Rapture has a few years to go before it occurs, but I'm still playing it safe and trying to be ready now. Remember, we have to consider the plus/minus 19 year factor from our chronology, and we are well within that range between now and the year 2028 - 2030.

Also, I'm not saying for sure God ordained exactly 4000 years for the Old Testament, it just seems like it is a possibility since 3997 is so close to that number already, and 40 is a significant number in the Bible. It fits. However, I'm not going to put God in a box and say He couldn't use a different number. What if it's 4007 Old Testament years, 1993 New Testament years, and those seven years needed for Israel to dispose of the weapons are consecutive? That would mean the Rapture could happen at any time.

Jesus told us not to let that day catch Christians off guard (Mark 13:23,33). This Scripture is one of the reasons I wanted to write this book now instead of later. There is no way to be sure the Rapture won't happen before 2030, so we should be prepared now. Jesus told His believers always to be watching for His return (Matthew 24:42).

Now, invariably, I know there will be some that will reject this whole timeline simply because God's Word says no one knows the day or the hour the Rapture will happen (Matthew 24:36). However, I'm not trying to predict the day or hour, and I'm not trying to predict the month or even the exact year. Saying the Rapture might occur between now and the year 2028-2030 is a far cry from trying to predict the day or the hour.

However, what this book is trying to do is understand the 'season' of Jesus' return at the Rapture. God's Word says there is nothing wrong with trying to understand when the 'season' of His return will be (1 Thessalonians 5:1-10). In fact, His Word encourages us to know that season and be ready (verse 6). God's Word also says the date of when that season will happen is set, will not be changed, and God proved it will occur by raising Jesus from the dead (Acts 17:31).

In chapter 1 we discussed why this is the last generation that will be on earth before Jesus returns, so we know we have to be close. We also talked about how much of what has been happening in the world today fulfills what Jesus said would occur shortly before His coming at the Rapture. So, after reading so many books on end times prophecy, endlessly studying God's Word, weighing different points of view, seeing how what is happening in the world today fulfills all the things Jesus said would occur before His return, and if the last generation from when Israel became a nation again lasted 80 years it would end about 6000 years from the creation of the world, this timeline seems correct to me.

If the next eight years come and go and the Rapture hasn't happened yet, then I'm wrong and it must be 100 years for the last generation before Jesus returns. If so, we can praise God that all non-believers have more time to repent and believe in Jesus to be saved; that is not a bad thing you know. However, things are accelerating very fast, and I believe most likely we will see either the Psalm 83 war occur within the next few years, or the Rapture will be the event that brings on the Psalm 83 war and the Tribulation. Agree or disagree, one thing is certain. The Rapture will occur, and you don't want to be left on earth for what is going to happen afterward.

****

I realize there may be many people that read this next chapter before the Rapture occurs. I hope the picture this chapter paints of what the world will be like for seven years after the Rapture will make them not want to miss the one opportunity they have to avoid having to be on earth during that time. However, I also realize this book will be around after the Rapture, and there will be many (possibly many more) who read this chapter after the Rapture has occurred as they will be looking for answers to what happened.

So, with that in mind, and since –

- Anyone reading this chapter after the Rapture has occurred will most likely skip the chapters before it (and rightly so)

- Since time will be much more important to them then than it is now

- Since this book was written in the hope that God would use it to bring many to faith in Jesus alone for their salvation both before and after the Rapture

- Since the Rapture could happen soon

The next chapter was written as if the Rapture has already occurred. For those reading this before the Rapture who are saved through faith in Jesus alone, praise God you will not be here when all this comes to pass. In addition, I implore you to go tell others who do not believe what is coming so they might come to the knowledge of saving faith and avoid the post-Rapture world as well.

For those reading this chapter that do not believe in salvation through faith in Jesus alone, my prayer is this will be the time when God's Spirit will reveal to you that these things will come to pass, especially whatever is written in God's Word. Those things are *guaranteed* to happen. I pray that as you read this chapter, you will be moved to receive Jesus Christ as your Lord and Savior.

6

The Rapture Has Come

"How much worse the punishment will be for those who have trampled on the Son of God, and have treated the blood of the covenant which made us holy as if it were common and unholy, and have insulted and distained the Holy Spirit who brings God's mercy to us…It is a terrible thing to fall into the hands of the living God."– Hebrews 10:29,31

So, it has happened.

Hundreds of millions of adults and well over a billion children all over the world have vanished in the blink of an eye. Anyone who was not taken possibly saw someone, or maybe a group of people, disappear right in front of them. Worse, maybe they saw their spouse or their children disappear before their very eyes. Words cannot express how sorry I am that they turned down God's offer of saving grace through faith in Jesus' death on the cross and resurrection from the dead. Most likely He offered His grace to them many times, not wanting them to go through all that will happen after the Rapture. However, they either rejected it every time, or thought they had already had it, but didn't.

Now the earth and everyone left in it has begun a time where God is going to pour out His wrath on an unbelieving world. Within three years, one-quarter of the people on earth will die from starvation, disease, war and natural disasters ordained by God (Revelation 6:8). Within five years, one half of the world's population will die (Rev 9:15), and if it lasted longer than seven years, there wouldn't be anyone left alive (Mark 13:19-20). The judgment of the God of the Bible is being poured out on a world that has overwhelmingly rejected him for over the entire course of the earth's 6000 years, and it is time for justice to be done.

The church age was ended when Jesus came back and took all true believers out of the world, just like the prophecies in the Bible said He would.

"For since we believe that Jesus died and was raised to life again, we also believe that when Jesus returns (at the Rapture), God will bring back

with Him (to heaven) the believers who have died. We tell you this directly from the Lord Jesus: We who are still living when the Lord returns will not meet Him ahead of those who have died. For the Lord Himself will come down from heaven with a commanding shout, with the voice of the archangel, and the trumpet call of God. First, the believers who have died will rise from their graves. Then, together with them, we who are still alive and remain on the earth (true believers in Jesus) will be caught up in the clouds to meet the Lord in the air. Then we will be with the Lord forever." – 1 Thessalonians 4:13-17

This is the main prophecy in the Bible about the Rapture of all true believers. There are a few others, but since it has already occurred, I don't think there needs to be a whole lot of explanation. This is what happened!

Anyone who was not taken had not repented of their sins and received saving faith through Jesus Christ. For anyone reading this after the Rapture, if you still have not repented and received Christ through faith in Him, you are under God's wrath and subject to His judgments. Before you do anything else, repent of your sins and receive forgiveness of them through faith in what Jesus did for you by taking the punishment you deserve upon Himself through His death on the cross and resurrection from the dead three days later.

If you are ready, pray a prayer like this –

Father God, forgive me of my sins. I realize I am a sinner before you in need of your saving grace through faith in your Son, Jesus Christ. For the sake of your Son, who died on the cross for my sins and was raised from the dead, please forgive me.

It doesn't have to be precisely those words. You just need to acknowledge your sins before God (repent) and confess to Him that you believe Jesus' death and resurrection from the dead is the only way you can be saved from your sin.

If you do this, you will not be under God's wrath anymore, but you will still have to remain on earth until Jesus comes back seven years after the Rapture. The only difference is, God will be punishing everyone else who hasn't repented of their sins.

Anyone who wasn't taken missed the chance not to have to be on the earth for those seven years, but they do have an opportunity to be a mouthpiece for God and tell others what happened and why everyone disappeared. That God is pouring out His wrath on an unbelieving world and there is only so much time left for them to receive forgiveness of their sins through faith in Jesus Christ. They can tell all their family and friends that are left and hopefully be the person God uses to bring them to saving faith. That's the Good News.

The bad news is, from the time the Rapture occurred until Jesus comes again seven years later, things are going to get progressively worse –

--- As much as a tenth of the adult population in the world vanished along with all children under a certain age of being accountable for choosing God's grace or rejecting it. Most likely that was all children under twelve years of age, including those not even born yet! God never says in the Bible that a child is not a child until he or she is born. God's Word says the opposite, that it is a child inside the womb –

*"At the sound of Mary's greeting, Elizabeth's **child** leaped within her, and Elizabeth was filled with the Holy Spirit. Elizabeth gave a glad cry and exclaimed to Mary, "God has blessed you above all women, and your **child** is blessed. Why am I so honored, that the mother of my Lord should visit me? When I heard your greeting, the baby in(side) my womb jumped for joy."* – Luke 1:41-44

Not only does the Bible use the word 'child' twice to describe the baby inside Elizabeth's womb, but the Greek word used for baby in those verses is the same word used in the Bible to describe babies that have already been born – brafos. God makes no distinction between the two. The Rapture has proved that God considers abortion the killing of a child.

--- The devastation from car crashes must have been indescribable. At any one time, there were hundreds of millions of cars on roads all over the world. If about ten percent of the vehicles on the roads crashed at the same time, millions of people must have been killed. We know this would have happened because according to the Association for Safe International Road Travel, over 400,000 people under the age of 25 were killed each year from car crashes in the world before the Rapture. If you include all those over that age too, millions died when all those cars crashed at the same time.

Tens of millions of cars, including thousands and thousands of semi-trucks, crashing all at once because the drivers were taken in the Rapture? I don't think that can be put into words. Anyone riding in a car whose driver was taken could have been killed as well as so many of the other drivers and passengers who were not taken but were caught in the pileups too. The loss of life must have been staggering. How could emergency services have possibly responded to that all over the world? No doubt many didn't die right away, but since emergency services could only respond to a small fraction of the accidents, many died from not being able to be taken to a hospital. How could they respond?

There were also emergency services needed for the millions of heart attacks that occurred from the shock of so many people and so many children disappearing. For all the fires that were started from car and airplane crashes igniting the surrounding vegetation or from people who left their stoves on or had a cigarette that dropped to the ground when they were taken which burned down who knows how many homes and buildings. The list goes on and on for things which the emergency services were needed. Don't forget, most roads were (still are?) impassible, so how were they going to get to where they needed to go? Also, there were many police officers, firefighters, ambulance drivers, hospital workers and others that could have helped, but they were taken in the Rapture.

--- No doubt there were dozens, possibly hundreds of airplane crashes all over the world too. At any time before the Rapture, there were over 10,000 planes in the air. If both pilots were taken and the aircraft wasn't on autopilot, it crashed. Even if the aircraft was on autopilot, once it ran out of fuel, it crashed.

--- The cleanup from all the cars and planes that crashed will take months. Many roads and highways were impassable for weeks or longer. If a person was driving or flying when the Rapture occurred, depending on how far away from home they were, it may have taken days or weeks to get home. If the Rapture occurred within the last month, maybe they still are not home yet.

--- Airports shut down for weeks. Not only because so many planes crashed but also because it's so hard for anyone to get to the airports with all the car accidents blocking so many roads and highways. This would mean for anyone who was traveling it could take weeks or months to get home. The impact of shut down airports and impassable roads for weeks or even months will affect the world in so many ways, and it's hard to describe. It will be a significant factor in the economic collapse that is underway.

--- The economic collapse will be covered in more detail later, but you can be sure there will be severe food and gas shortages. Long term blackouts and cell phone outages that make it impossible to contact family members or friends. Internet services, something everyone had come to depend on will be unavailable for a long period of time and will probably never be like it was before the Rapture. The negative economic impact of that alone is hard to visualize. The internet was responsible for putting who knows how many thousands of retailers out of business, and those retailers are not available now when they are needed more than ever.

--- The looting in America and around the world must be on a scale that no one could have ever imagined. In America, the police can't stop it, and the military can't stop it. The military has been decimated. There was a higher percentage of people taken from the military than ten percent, and I can guarantee you that. A study from 2005 showed as much as 40% of the American military considered themselves evangelical Christians, and evangelical Christians were the overwhelming majority of Christians taken in the Rapture. Why did that happen? Because evangelical Christians were the ones most likely to believe what God revealed in the Bible. That faith in Jesus was their only hope for being saved and to be taken in the Rapture, whether they knew about the Rapture or not.

Those reading this chapter may have read the chapters before it or may have skipped them now that the Rapture has occurred, but many people may have noticed that not everyone who claimed to be a Christian was taken. In fact, few people who claimed to be Christians were taken. Why was not everyone who claimed to be a Christian taken? They were not taken because they were not true Christians.

For more information about who was a true Christian and who wasn't, see the chapter about who would be taken in the Rapture and who would not, as well as the appendix at the back of the book. However, the short explanation is – They claimed to be Christians, but their actions revealed whether or not they truly believed in their heart (really had faith) that through Jesus' sinless life, death on the cross and resurrection from the dead, that they could receive forgiveness for their sins against God.

Their actions before the Rapture that showed they did not have true saving faith were revealed to the one who judges all people…Jesus Christ.

"For the Father (God) judges no one, but has given all judgment to the Son (Jesus), that all may honor the Son, just as they honor the Father." – John 5:22, English Standard Version Bible

Now since God the Father and Jesus are the same one true God –

"I and the Father are One." – John 10:30, ESV Bible

"Whoever has seen Me has seen the Father." – John 14:9, ESV Bible

Since the Bible also says no one can hide from God (which includes their actions) –

"Can anyone hide from Me in a secret place? Am I not everywhere in all the heavens and earth? says the Lord." – Jeremiah 23:24

"Nothing in all creation is hidden from God. Everything is naked and exposed before His eyes, and He is the one to whom we are accountable." – Hebrews 4:13

Then wouldn't Jesus know if a person was not a true believer in Him, and not take them when He came in the Rapture? Of course, He knew…and did not take them.

No one was taken who believed they knew better than what God revealed in the Bible – plainly revealed! That faith alone, in Jesus Christ alone, was and still is the only way to be saved; that no amount of good works can ever be done by anyone to save themselves.

"God saved you by His grace when you believed (in Jesus Christ). You can't take credit for this; it is a gift from God. Salvation is not a reward for the good things we've done, so none of us can boast about it (that we helped save ourselves)." – Ephesians 2:8-9

No one was taken who believed there was more than one way to be saved. Jesus said –

"I am the way, the truth, and the life, no one can come to (God) the Father except through (faith in) me." – John 14:6

No one was taken who believed all religions worship the same God.

"Believe in me and understand that I alone am God. There is no other God. There ever has been, and there never will be. I, yes, I am the Lord, and there is no other Savior." – Isaiah 43:10-11

God's Word said these people got it wrong, and the Rapture of all true believers has proven it –

- The Popes of the Roman Catholic Church

- Muhammad, founder of Islam

- Joseph Smith Jr, founder of Mormonism

- Charles Taze Russell, founder of Jehovah's Witness

- Sun Myung Moon, founder of the Unification church

God's Word said these religions got it wrong, and the Rapture of all true believers has proven it.

- Buddhism

- Hinduism

- Hare Krishna

- Taoism

- Judaism

- Deism

- Agnosticism

- Unitarianism

- Freemasonry

- Shinto

- Wicca

- Atheism

- Naturalism

These are not all the false prophets and false religions in the world, but any person that claims what God revealed in His Word the Bible was wrong, and what that person says is right, is a false prophet. Any religion that says human beings can or must contribute to their salvation, or that salvation requires faith in Jesus *plus* anything, is a false religion. Again, the Rapture has proven this.

Anyone still following any of these false prophets or false religions should repent of their sins against the One true God and receive forgiveness through faith in the life, death, and resurrection of Jesus Christ alone. What more evidence does a person need that it is the only way to have eternal life! (If you want to see God's Word regarding any or all of these false religions, and how God's Word says they are wrong, you can read about them in the appendix.)

Sadly, many false prophets, like the Pope, are still on earth. Many of the leaders of all the false religions will not accept that they were wrong. So they, along with other leaders of the world will have to come up with some explanation for what happened; why hundreds of millions of adults and over a billion children disappeared all at once. There has been much speculation on how that might be done. However, I believe the two most plausible explanations that most of the people of the world will buy into (or have already) will be either an abduction by aliens or whatever the false apparition of Mary (which is demonic) tells the world. Perhaps the false apparition of Mary did tell the world they were abducted by aliens.

The last thing Satan wants is for millions and millions of people to come to saving faith in Jesus Christ as a result of the Rapture. The good news is, it will happen…and it is happening. God's Word says so many will be saved during the Tribulation that they cannot be counted –

"After this I saw a vast crowd, too great to count, from every nation and tribe and people and language, standing in front of the throne and before the Lamb (Jesus). They were clothed in white robes and held palm branches in their hands, and they were shouting with a great roar, "Salvation comes from our God who sits on the throne and from the Lamb!" – Revelation 7:9-10

"Then one of the twenty-four elders asked me, "Who are these who are clothed in white? Where did they come from?" And I said to him, "Sir, you are the one who knows." Then he said to me, "These are the ones who died in the great tribulation. They have washed their robes in the blood of the Lamb and made them white." – Revelation 7:13-14

However, Satan is going to try to stop it, so there will be (or already was) an explanation given for what happened at the Rapture. Do not believe it! Whether the people who disappeared were said to have been taken by aliens to the dark side of the moon or somewhere else in the universe, or whatever the demonic apparition of Mary tells the world, it is not true. God delivered on yet another promise from His Word!

There are several more to come. Yes, the Rapture precedes the seven years where God pours out His wrath on an unbelieving world, but it also is the time when the Antichrist is revealed, and he will lead the world into global war and destruction.

His coming and the timing of that coming are foretold –

"Don't be fooled by what they say (false prophets and false teachers). For that day (the return of Jesus to the earth) will not come until there is a great rebellion against God and the (Antichrist) is revealed – the one who brings destruction. He will exalt himself and defy everything that people call god and every object of worship. He will even sit in the temple of God, claiming that he is God." – 2 Thessalonians 2:3-4

"And you know what is holding him back (God is), for he can be revealed only when his time comes. For this lawlessness is already at work secretly, and it will remain secret until the One who is holding it back steps out of the way. Then the (Antichrist) will be revealed, but the Lord Jesus will slay him with the breath of his mouth and destroy him by the splendor of his coming. This man will come to do the work of Satan with counterfeit power and signs and miracles. He will use every kind of evil deception to fool those on their way to destruction because they refuse to love and accept the truth that would save them." – 2 Thessalonians 2:6-12

The Antichrist has probably been revealed already. Once the Rapture happens, it will not be long before the prophecy about him appearing is fulfilled (Revelation 6:2). He is the one to whom ten of the world's leaders will give their power (Revelation 17:12-13). Why would they do that? Well, two reasons. We've already talked about some of the things that have happened since the Rapture occurred –

Millions of people killed in car and airplane crashes. Many died from heart attacks and many more from the impossibility of emergency services responding to all that, plus all the fires that were started that burned so many thousands, possibly millions, of homes and buildings all over the world. Severe food and gas shortages everywhere due to the complete breakdown of transportation by roads and by air, with police and militaries not being able to stop the looting of what was left. The internet, which the world had come to rely on for so much of its commerce, is now down or has been made ineffective.

All this will lead (or has already led) to a complete and total worldwide economic collapse of a magnitude that is beyond comprehension. When all these factors come together at once, the negative impact on the global economy will be catastrophic –

- Hundreds of millions of adults taken out of the workforce at the same time

- Over a billion children are gone. Any business that relies on or is geared towards young children will close

- Hundreds of millions of parents that lost children will stop working from grief or because there is no one left in the family to have to support

- Hundreds of millions of people are staying home to protect their houses, their cars, and their families from the looting and lawlessness that abounds everywhere

- All school teachers in the whole world, preschool through junior high are out of work, and many high school teachers too

- Major transportation problems on roads and by plane

- Retail stores, food stores, restaurants and gas stations cannot be resupplied

- Internet orders cannot be processed. Even if they can, delivery problems are delaying or preventing deliveries altogether

Hundreds of millions of home loans, car loans and credit card loans not being repaid to banks anymore due to –

- Hundreds of millions of adults taken in the Rapture

- Parents that lost children have stopped working

- So many that cannot leave the house due to looting and lawlessness

- Out of work construction workers all over the world. Most projects have stopped due to lack of materials that can be supplied

- The internet is down, or not as effective a method of transferring money as it used to be

- Businesses that have either gone out of business, had all their products stolen by looting, or now can't generate enough income to pay their loans back

This will result in the collapse of the entire world banking system which will also mean –

- People will go to banks to get their money, but there's not enough cash. Most banks had less than 5% of cash on hand for total deposits *before* the Rapture

- All stock markets will be cut in half or even by two thirds, possibly in a matter of weeks

- Hundreds of millions of pensions that rely on the stock markets going up? Wiped out and gone

- Hundreds of millions of 401K's that retirees rely on? Wiped out and gone

- Social Security payments that seniors depend on? Wiped out and gone

This is just a partial list of what has happened, is happening, and will happen as a result of the Rapture. The leaders of the world are more than happy to give their power to the Antichrist who claims to have the answers to the catastrophic economic collapse. There are also wars that have erupted all over the world as well. Leaders are anxious to find peace, and it will appear the Antichrist is the person that can do all that.

But the main reason they will give their power to the Antichrist is that God told them to. God always has been, and still is in control of everything that happens on the earth –

"For God has put a plan into their minds, a plan that will carry out His purposes. They will agree to give their authority to the (Antichrist), and so the words of God will be fulfilled." – Revelation 17:17

The Antichrist will conquer the world through peaceful means for a while, as indicated by the prophecy showing him on a white horse and having a bow but no arrows –

"I looked, and there before me was a white horse! Its rider held a bow (no arrows), and he was given a crown, and he rode out as a rider to conquer, bent on conquest." – Revelation 6:2

However, halfway through the seven years where God is pouring out His wrath on an unbelieving world, the Antichrist will unleash total war over the entire earth.

The first thing he will do is end the sacrifices at the rebuilt temple in Israel and claim that he is God –

"He will oppose and will exalt himself over everything that is called God or is worshiped, so that he sets himself up in God's temple, proclaiming himself to be God." – 2 Thessalonians 2:4, NIV

From this point on, the Bible calls the Antichrist 'the Beast' and Satan gives the Beast all his power –

"The dragon (Satan) stood on the shore of the sea. And I saw a Beast coming out of the sea... The dragon gave the Beast his power and his throne and great authority." – Revelation 13:1a-2b

At some point, the Antichrist will receive what looks like a fatal wound (possible assassination attempt?) and will appear to have been killed. However, he will come alive again, and this will cause many in the world to worship him and Satan –

"I saw that one of the heads of the Beast seemed wounded beyond recovery—but the fatal wound was healed! The whole world marveled at this miracle and gave allegiance to the Beast. They worshiped the dragon for giving the beast such power, and they also worshiped the Beast." – Revelation 13:3-4

Worship from people is something Satan has wanted all along. He even wanted Jesus to worship him (Matthew 4:9). Somehow people will know where the Antichrist's power is coming from. Satan will make sure of that.

There will also be a false prophet (called a second beast) that will be given power by God to do miracles and signs and wonders, even to make fire come down from heaven –

"Then I saw a second beast, coming out of the earth. It had two horns like a lamb, but it spoke like a dragon. It exercised all the authority of the first beast on its behalf; and made the earth and its inhabitants worship the first beast, whose fatal wound had been healed. It performed great signs, even causing fire to come down from heaven to the earth in full view of the people." – Revelation 13:11-13

Because of these miracles, the false prophet will deceive the world, and he will order the inhabitants of the earth to set up an image of the Antichrist to be worshipped. He will even be given power by God to make the image come alive and speak to deceive the people of the earth further –

"And with all the miracles he was allowed to perform on behalf of the first beast, he deceived all the people who belong to this world. He ordered the people to make a great statue of the first beast, who was fatally wounded and then came back to life. He was then permitted to give life to this statue so that it could speak. Then the statue of the beast commanded that anyone refusing to worship it must die." – Revelation 13:14-15

Do not be deceived! God is in control!

God is allowing this so that all who will not believe in the truth of God's grace through faith in Jesus, all who delight in wickedness, that they will believe the lie (that the Antichrist is god) and will worship the Antichrist and be condemned –

"The coming of the (Antichrist) will be in accordance with how Satan works. He will use all sorts of displays of power through signs and wonders that serve the lie, and all the ways that wickedness deceives those who are

perishing. They perish because they refused to love the truth and so be saved. For this reason, God sends them a powerful delusion so that they will believe the lie and so that all will be condemned who have not believed the truth but have delighted in wickedness." – 2 Thessalonians 2:9-12

This false prophet will also make everyone receive the mark of the Antichrist, his name or his number (666), on their right hand or their forehead and anyone who does not take the mark will not be able to buy or sell anything –

"He required everyone—small and great, rich and poor, free and slave—to be given a mark on the right hand or the forehead. No one could buy or sell anything without that mark, which was either the name of the Beast or the number representing his name. Wisdom is needed here. Let the one with understanding solve the meaning of the number of the Beast, for it is the number of a man. His number is 666." – Revelation 13:16-18

Do not take this mark!

Do not worship the Antichrist!

Anyone who takes this mark or worships the Antichrist has assured themselves an eternity of suffering in the lake of fire. God will even send an angel to announce this to all the people left in the world –

"A third angel followed them, shouting, "Anyone who worships the beast and his statue or who accepts his mark on the forehead or on the hand, must drink the wine of God's anger. It has been poured full strength into God's cup of wrath. They will be tormented with fire and burning sulfur in the presence of the holy angels and (Jesus). The smoke of their torment will rise forever and ever, and they will have no relief day or night, for they have worshiped the beast and his statue and have accepted the mark of his name." – Revelation 14:9-11

God already sent, and will send, more warnings during these seven years for people to turn to him through faith in Jesus Christ alone. The Rapture was a warning that His judgment has come. However, His true believers were not appointed to His wrath and were taken out of the world before the Tribulation started.

"Since you have kept my command to endure patiently (in faith), I will also keep you from the hour of trial that is going to come on the whole world to test the inhabitants of the earth." – Revelation 3:10, NIV Bible

Another warning from God are His two witnesses who appeared in Jerusalem right after the Rapture and for 1,260 days (42 months) are telling people to repent and turn to Jesus for salvation. This is according to Bible prophecy –

"And I will appoint my two witnesses, and they will prophesy for 1,260 days, clothed in sackcloth." – Revelation 11:3, NIV Bible

They cannot be harmed for those three and a half years. Anyone that tries to harm them will be killed by fire, and they are given power by God to stop the rain, turn water to blood, and bring plagues to the earth –

"If anyone tries to harm them, fire comes from their mouths and devours their enemies. This is how anyone who wants to harm them must die. They have the power to shut up the heavens so that it will not rain during the time they are prophesying, and they have power to turn the waters into blood and to strike the earth with every kind of plague as often as they want." – Revelation 11:5-6, NIV Bible

After 42 months, around the time the Antichrist declares himself to be god, he kills the two witnesses (Rev 11:7). Their bodies lie in the street for three and a half days while the whole world sees them, and people on the earth rejoice that they are dead because they were causing great trouble to an unbelieving earth –

"For three and a half days some from every people, tribe, language and nation will gaze on their bodies and refuse them burial. The inhabitants of the earth will gloat over them and will celebrate by sending each other gifts, because these two prophets had tormented those who live on the earth." – Revelation 11:9-10, NIV Bible

However, after the three and a half days, God brings the two witnesses to life again, striking terror in all who see it. God takes them to heaven in the same way he took everyone else in the Rapture, using the same words as before, 'Come up here." –

"But after three and a half days, God breathed life into them, and they stood up! Terror struck all who were staring at them. Then a loud voice from heaven called to the two prophets, "Come up here!" And they rose to heaven in a cloud as their enemies watched." – Revelation 11:11-12

Anyone who is reading this while the two witnesses are still alive, listen to them! They are God's messengers. Repent and turn to Jesus for the forgiveness of your sins!

If the two witnesses were already killed and taken back to heaven, then listen to the 144,000 Jewish priests that God has sent all over the world. They came to saving faith through the testimony of the two witnesses, and God has sent them to spread the message of His saving grace through faith in Jesus Christ alone. Because of the testimonies of the two witnesses and the 144,000 Jewish priests, there are so many people from every nation coming to saving faith in Jesus that by the end of the last three and a half years of the Tribulation, they cannot be counted.

"After this I looked, and there before me was a great multitude that no one could count, from every nation, tribe, people and language, standing before the throne and before the Lamb. They were wearing white robes and were holding palm branches in their hands. And they cried out in a loud voice: "Salvation belongs to our God, who sits on the throne, and to the Lamb." – Revelation 7:9-10, NIV Bible

"...Then one of the elders asked me, "These in white robes—who are they, and where did they come from?" I answered, "Sir, you know." And he said, "These are they who have come out of the great tribulation; they have washed their robes and made them white in the blood of the Lamb. Therefore, "they are before the throne of God and serve Him day and night in his temple; and He who sits on the throne will shelter them with his presence. Never again will they hunger; never again will they thirst. The sun will not beat down on them, nor any scorching heat. For the Lamb at the center of the throne will be their shepherd; He will lead them to springs of living water. And God will wipe away every tear from their eyes." – Revelation 7:13-17, NIV Bible

Those not taken in the Rapture have a chance to be part of this glorious picture the Bible describes! If they repent and receive forgiveness for their sins through faith in Jesus Christ alone.

When the Antichrist declares he is god, Satan will then try to destroy Israel. However, God will protect them for the next three and a half years –

"She (Israel) gave birth to a son (Jesus)...And her child was snatched away from the dragon (Satan) and was caught up to God and to his throne

(taken back to heaven after Jesus rose again from the dead). And the woman fled into the wilderness, where God had prepared a place to care for her for 1,260 days (three and a half years)." – Revelation 12:5-6

And when Satan realizes he cannot destroy all the people of Israel, he will make war on the rest of the believers throughout the world –

"...he (Satan) pursued the woman who had given birth to the male child. But she was given two wings like those of a great eagle so she could fly to the place prepared for her in the wilderness. There she would be cared for and protected from the dragon for a time, times, and half a time (three and a half years)...And the dragon was angry at the woman and declared war against the rest of her children – all who keep God's commandments and maintain their testimony for Jesus."–Revelation 12:13b-14, 17

Satan will make one last attempt to prevent his final defeat at the hands of Jesus –

"Then the devil, who had deceived them, was thrown into the fiery lake of burning sulfur joining the beast and the false prophet. There they will be tormented day and night forever and ever." – Revelation 20:10

Ultimately, Satan was defeated when Jesus died on the cross and rose again from the dead –

"Inasmuch then as the children have partaken of flesh and blood, He Himself likewise shared in the same, that through death He might destroy him who had the power of death, that is, the devil." – Hebrews 2:14, New King James Version Bible

However, Satan is going to try to stop his being thrown into the lake of fire by unleashing global war through the Antichrist. This is one of the reasons Jesus said if the Tribulation lasted more than seven years, no one would be left alive (Matthew 24:22).

However, that is not the only reason that if the Tribulation lasted longer than seven years no one would be left alive. For the entire seven years, God is pouring out His wrath on an unbelieving world in a series of 21 judgments that get progressively worse. Here are the judgments, in order, with a brief explanation –

The first judgment unleashed the Antichrist to conquer the world –

"I watched as the Lamb (Jesus) opened the first of the seven seals...I looked, and there before me was a white horse! Its rider held a bow, and he

was given a crown, and he rode out as a conqueror bent on conquest." – Revelation 6:1-2, NIV Bible

The second judgment brings wars all over the world –

"When the Lamb broke the second seal…Then another horse appeared, a red one. Its rider was given a mighty sword and the authority to take peace from the earth. And there was war and slaughter everywhere." – Revelation 6:3-4

The third judgment brings economic collapse and famine –

"When the Lamb broke the third seal…I looked up and saw a black horse, and its rider was holding a pair of scales in his hand. And I heard a voice from among the four living beings say, "A loaf of wheat bread or three loaves of barley will cost a day's pay." – Revelation 6:5-6

The fourth judgment adds famine and disease. By this time, one-fourth of the people on the earth will have died –

"When the Lamb opened the fourth seal…I looked, and there before me was a pale horse! Its rider was named Death, and Hades was following close behind him. They were given power over a fourth of the earth to kill by sword, famine and plague…" – Revelation 6:7-8, NIV Bible

The fifth judgment brings a promise from God that He will avenge those who have been martyred for their faith in God and Jesus Christ –

"When he opened the fifth seal, I saw under the altar the souls of those who had been slain because of the word of God and the testimony they had maintained. They called out in a loud voice, "How long, Sovereign Lord, holy and true until you judge the inhabitants of the earth and avenge our blood?" Then each of them was given a white robe, and they were told to wait a little longer, until the full number of their fellow servants, their brothers, and sisters, were killed just as they had been." – Revelation 6:9-11, NIV Bible

The sixth judgment brings a huge earthquake that moves mountains and islands out of place, the sun is darkened, the moon turned blood red, and stars fall from the sky –

"I watched as the Lamb broke the sixth seal, and there was a great earthquake. The sun became as dark as black cloth, and the moon became as red as blood. Then the stars of the sky fell to the earth like green figs falling from a tree shaken by a strong wind. The sky was rolled up like a

scroll, and all of the mountains and islands were moved from their places."
– Revelation 6:12-14

At this point, everyone knows God is pouring out His wrath on the earth–

"Then everyone—the kings of the earth, the rulers, the generals, the wealthy, the powerful, and every slave and free person—all hid themselves in the caves and among the rocks of the mountains. And they cried to the mountains and the rocks, "Fall on us and hide us from the face of the one who sits on the throne and from the wrath of the Lamb. For the great day of their wrath has come, and who is able to survive?" – Revelation 6:15-17

The seventh judgment brings thunder, lightning and another great earthquake and unleashes the next seven judgments on the world –

"When the Lamb broke the seventh seal on the scroll…I saw the seven angels who stand before God, and they were given seven trumpets. Then another angel with a gold incense burner came and stood at the altar. And a great amount of incense was given to him to mix with the prayers of God's people as an offering on the gold altar before the throne…Then the angel filled the incense burner with fire from the altar and threw it down upon the earth, and thunder crashed, lightning flashed, and there was a terrible earthquake." – Revelation 8:1-3,5

The eight judgment brings hail and fire down upon the earth, and a third of the earth is burned up –

"The first angel sounded his trumpet, and there came hail and fire mixed with blood, and it was hurled down on the earth. A third of the earth was burned up, a third of the trees were burned up, and all the green grass was burned up." – Revelation 8:7, NIV Bible

The ninth judgment turns one-third of the oceans and seas to blood. And one-third of all living creatures in the seas die, and one-third of all ships are destroyed –

"Then the second angel blew his trumpet, and a great mountain of fire was thrown into the sea. One-third of the water in the sea became blood, one-third of all things living in the sea died, and one-third of all the ships on the sea were destroyed." – Revelation 8:8-9

The tenth judgment turns one-third of all rivers and lakes into undrinkable water that can kill someone if they drink it –

"Then the third angel blew his trumpet, and a great star fell from the sky, burning like a torch. It fell on one-third of the rivers and on the springs of water. The name of the star was Bitterness. It made one-third of the water bitter, and many people died from drinking the bitter water." – Revelation 8:10-11

The eleventh judgment turns one-third of the sun, one-third of the moon, and one-third of the stars into darkness –

"Then the fourth angel blew his trumpet, and one-third of the sun was struck, and one-third of the moon, and one-third of the stars, and they became dark. And one-third of the day was dark, and also one-third of the night." – Revelation 8:12

The twelfth judgment brings locusts that can sting like scorpions and they will only sting those who have not repented and received forgiveness for their sins through faith in Jesus Christ alone. This will go on for five months. People will wish to die but will not be able to –

"Then the fifth angel blew his trumpet, and I saw a star that had fallen to earth from the sky… smoke poured out as though from a huge furnace, and the sunlight and air turned dark from the smoke. Then locusts came from the smoke and descended on the earth, and they were given power to sting like scorpions. They were told not to harm the grass or plants or trees, but only the people who did not have the seal of God on their foreheads. They were told not to kill them but to torture them for five months with pain like the pain of a scorpion sting. In those days people will seek death but will not find it. They will long to die, but death will flee from them!" – Revelation 9:1-6

The thirteenth judgment releases four angels who kill a third of all people left on the earth –

"Then the sixth angel blew his trumpet…And the voice said to the sixth angel who held the trumpet, "Release the four angels who are bound at the great Euphrates River." Then the four angels who had been prepared for this hour and day and month and year were turned loose to kill one-third of all the people on earth." – Revelation 9:13-15

Despite all the judgments up to this point, most of the people left on earth still will not repent of their sins –*"But the people who did not die in these plagues still refused to repent of their evil deeds and turn to God. They continued to worship demons and idols made of gold, silver, bronze, stone, and wood—idols that can neither see nor hear nor walk! And they did not repent of their murders or their witchcraft or their sexual immorality or their thefts."* – Revelation 9:20-21

The fourteenth judgment brings thunder, lightning, an earthquake, and a great hailstorm over all the earth and unleashes the last seven judgments of God on the world –

"Then the seventh angel blew his trumpet, and there were loud voices shouting in heaven: "The world has now become the Kingdom of our Lord and of his Christ, and He will reign forever and ever." The twenty-four elders sitting on their thrones before God fell with their faces to the ground and worshiped him. And they said, "We give thanks to you, Lord God, the Almighty, the One who is and who always was, for now, you have assumed your great power and have begun to reign. The nations were filled with wrath, but now the time of your wrath has come. It is time to judge the dead and reward your servants the prophets, as well as your holy people, and all who fear your name, from the least to the greatest. It is time to destroy all who have caused destruction on the earth."

Then, in heaven, the Temple of God was opened, and the Ark of his covenant could be seen inside the Temple. Lightning flashed, thunder crashed and roared, and there was an earthquake and a terrible hailstorm." – Revelation 11:15-19

The fifteenth judgment brings painful sores on all who have the mark of the Antichrist and worshipped his image –

"Then I heard a loud voice from the temple saying to the seven angels, "Go, pour out the seven bowls of God's wrath on the earth." The first angel went and poured out his bowl on the land, and ugly, festering sores broke out on the people who had the mark of the beast and worshiped its image." – Revelation 16:1-2, NIV Bible

The sixteenth judgment turns the rest of the oceans and seas into blood, and every living creature in them dies –

"The second angel poured out his bowl on the sea, and it turned into blood like that of a dead person, and every living thing in the sea died." – Revelation 16:3, NIV Bible

The seventeenth judgment turns all the rivers and lakes into blood, and every living thing in them will die too –

"The third angel poured out his bowl on the rivers and springs of water, and they became blood." – Revelation 16:4, NIV Bible

This is done because of all the shedding of the blood of God's believers throughout all of history –

"And I heard the angel who had authority over all water saying, "You are just, O Holy One, who is and who always was, because you have sent these judgments. Since they shed the blood of your holy people and your prophets, you have given them blood to drink. It is their just reward." – Revelation 16:5-6

The eighteenth judgment intensifies the heat of the sun and people are scorched by the intense heat –

"The fourth angel poured out his bowl on the sun, and the sun was allowed to scorch people with fire." – Revelation 16:8, NIV Bible

Most people will still refuse to repent of their sins and take hold of God's saving grace through faith in Jesus Christ alone –

"They were seared by the intense heat and they cursed the name of God, who had control over these plagues, but they refused to repent and glorify him." – Revelation 16:9, NIV Bible

The nineteenth judgment will plunge the kingdom of the Antichrist into total darkness and those who have his mark or worship his image, who are still identified by the sores on their bodies, will chew their own tongues because of the state of agony they are in –

"The fifth angel poured out his bowl on the throne of the Beast, and its kingdom was plunged into darkness. People gnawed their tongues in agony" – Revelation 16:10, NIV Bible

The twentieth judgment unleashes evil spirits that will gather all the leaders of the world and bring their armies to Armageddon so that they may be destroyed at the coming of Jesus Christ -

"The sixth angel poured out his bowl on the great river Euphrates, and its water was dried up to prepare the way for the kings from the East. Then I saw three impure spirits that looked like frogs…They are demonic spirits that perform signs, and they go out to the kings of the whole world, to gather them for the battle on the great day of God Almighty." –Revelation 16:12-14, NIV Bible

The twenty-first judgment beings thunder, lightning and the biggest earthquake ever upon the earth. Whole cities collapse, mountains are leveled, every island falls into the seas of blood, and hailstones as heavy as seventy-five pounds rain down on the earth –

"Then the seventh angel poured out his bowl into the air and a mighty shout came from the throne in the Temple, saying, "It is finished!" Then the thunder crashed and rolled, and lightning flashed. A great earthquake struck—the worst since people were placed on the earth. The great city of Babylon split into three sections, and the cities of many nations fell into heaps of rubble…And every island disappeared, and all the mountains were leveled. There was a terrible hailstorm, and hailstones weighing as much as seventy-five pounds fell from the sky onto the people below." – Revelation 16:17-21

Most of the people who are left on earth still will not repent of their sins–

"They cursed God because of the terrible plague of the hailstorm." – Revelation 16:21b

And then…Jesus will return

"I saw heaven standing open and there before me was a white horse, whose rider is called Faithful and True. With justice He judges and wages war. His eyes are like blazing fire, and on His head are many crowns. He has a name written on Him that no one knows but He himself. He is dressed in a robe dipped in blood, and His name is the Word of God." – Revelation 19: 11-13

Everyone who died with saving faith and went to heaven since the time that Jesus was crucified and rose again, until He came at the Rapture, they all will come down from heaven with Him at this time –

"The armies of heaven were following Him, riding on white horses and dressed in fine linen, white and clean." – Revelation 19:14, NIV Bible

Jesus will defeat the Antichrist, the false prophet and all the armies of the world gathered against Him –

"Coming out of His mouth is a sharp sword with which to strike down the nations…He treads the winepress of the fury of the wrath of God Almighty. On His robe and on His thigh, He has this name written: KING OF KINGS AND LORD OF LORDS." – Revelation 19:15-16, NIV Bible

"Then I saw the (Antichrist) and the kings of the earth and their armies gathered together to wage war against the rider on the horse and His army. But the (Antichrist) was captured, and with it the false prophet who had performed the signs on its behalf. With these signs he had deluded those who had received the mark of the beast and worshiped its image. The two of them were thrown alive into the fiery lake of burning sulfur. The rest were killed with the sword coming out of the mouth of the rider on the horse, and all the birds gorged themselves on their flesh." – Revelation 19:19-21, NIV Bible

Then Jesus will throw Satan into a bottomless pit for a thousand years and usher in His millennial reign on earth –

"And I saw an angel coming down out of heaven, having the key to the Abyss and holding in his hand a great chain. He seized the dragon, that ancient serpent, who is the devil, or Satan, and bound him for a thousand years. He threw him into the Abyss, and locked and sealed it over him, to keep him from deceiving the nations anymore until the thousand years were ended." – Revelation 20:1-3, NIV Bible

Then everyone who took Jesus as their Lord and Savior after the Rapture, but was killed before Jesus came back, will be raised to life again and will reign with Jesus –

"And I saw the souls of those who had been beheaded because of their testimony about Jesus and because of the word of God. They had not worshiped the beast or its image and had not received its mark on their foreheads or their hands. They came to life and reigned with Christ a thousand years." – Revelation 20:4b, NIV Bible

Jesus Christ will win. It is *guaranteed.*

If you still haven't repented of your sins and received forgiveness through faith in Jesus Christ alone, please do so now! If the Antichrist has already declared himself to be god and you haven't taken his mark, repent of your sins now and receive forgiveness through faith in Jesus Christ alone. Only through His life, death on the cross, and resurrection can you be saved.

Most of the verses from God's Word were provided in this chapter because I'm fully aware there will come a time during the Tribulation where holding a Bible will be a death sentence. Although it was still a death sentence to have a Bible in certain countries before the Rapture, I encouraged readers to reference a Bible.

However, soon after the Rapture and certainly after the Antichrist declares himself to be god, it will be a death sentence to have a Bible anywhere in the world. It is possible that Bibles will be hard to find because the Antichrist and other leaders may set out to destroy every copy they can. Who knows, they may set out to destroy every copy of this book as well. Along with any book that has the message of God's saving grace through faith in Jesus Christ alone.

I want to finish this book by talking about some of the things that are waiting for all those who came to saving faith through Jesus alone. We have already seen so many of God's promises come true through the Rapture and the prophecies of His judgments on the people of the earth. We can be sure the promises in the Bible that describe what is waiting for those who will spend eternal life with God and Jesus are true as well.

The Bible is the divinely revealed Word of God, and it is a story from beginning to end. A story about the incredible, unfathomable love of God for all the people He created. Beginning with Adam and Eve, and for everyone throughout all of history, as He made each one of them in their mothers' wombs –

"For you created my inmost being; you knit me together in my mother's womb." – Psalm 139:13, NIV Bible

It is a story about God's plan to restore everything to the way He intended from the beginning. A restoration of all the things He made –

"And the one sitting on the throne said, "Look, I am making everything new!" And then He said to me, "Write this down, for what I tell you is trustworthy and true."–Revelation 21:5

A restoration of His desire to have eternal relationships with His greatest creation; the ones He created in His own image, man and woman –

"And I heard a loud voice from the throne saying, "Look! God's dwelling place is now among the people, and he will dwell with them. They will be his people, and God himself will be with them and be their God. 'He will wipe every tear from their eyes. There will be no more death' or mourning or crying or pain, for the old order of things has passed away." – Revelation 21:3-4, NIV Bible

This would include anyone who died with saving faith from the beginning of time, anyone who was taken in the Rapture, and anyone who repented of their sins and received saving faith through Jesus Christ alone after the Rapture occurred.

The promises God reveals in His Word for what those eternal relationships will look like are impossible to imagine. The Bible even says we can't imagine it all –

"No eye has seen, no ear has heard, and no mind has imagined what God has prepared for those who love Him." – 1 Corinthians 2:9

However, God did reveal quite a bit in the Bible of what that might look like. To make sure this book stays consistent with the Bible being a message of hope, we should end it by going over some of those promises. There are promises that are taking place in the current heaven right now (above) and promises that will take place when heaven moves to earth after Jesus comes back.

In the current heaven –

Even though the physical body of a believer died, it seems so real they cannot tell if they are still in their physical body or not. The apostle Paul was taken to heaven briefly when he almost died by stoning, and he said these words – *"I was caught up to the third heaven fourteen years ago. Whether I was in my body or out of my body, I do not know—only God knows."* – 2 Corinthians 12:2

A person in heaven is the same person that they were on earth. We know this because even those who are saved through faith in Christ will still have to stand before Jesus and give an account of their life –

"For we must all appear before the judgment seat of Christ, so that each of us may receive what is due us for the things done while in the body, whether good or bad." – 2 Corinthians 5:10, NIV Bible

This verse talks about receiving rewards in heaven for those who belonged to Jesus Christ while on earth. A person who went to heaven has to be the same person he or she was while on earth. Otherwise, he or she is not the same person who is receiving those rewards in heaven!

There are many children there. (See the chapter of this book about children taken in the Rapture)

The soul will find rest in heaven –

"For all who have entered into God's rest have rested from their labors, just as God did after creating the world." – Hebrews 4:10

There are millions and millions of angels in heaven –

"Then I looked and heard the voice of many angels, numbering thousands upon thousands, and ten thousand times ten thousand. They encircled the throne and the living creatures and the elders." – Revelation 5:11, NIV Bible

A person will meet their guardian angels in heaven –

"If you make the LORD your refuge, if you make the Most High your shelter (through faith in Jesus)...(then) He will order his angels to protect you wherever you go." – Psalm 91:9, 11

A person has a place to live in heaven above –

"In My Father's house are many mansions; if it were not so, I would have told you. I go to prepare a place for you." – John 14:2, NKJV Bible

These 'mansions' are currently in the city in heaven called 'New Jerusalem.' Here is how the apostle John described the city when he saw it –

"It shone with the glory of God and sparkled like a precious stone—like jasper as clear as crystal. The city wall was broad and high, with twelve gates guarded by twelve angels. There were three gates on each side—east, north, south, and west." – Revelation 21:11-13

"The angel who talked to me held in his hand a gold measuring stick to measure the city, its gates, and its wall. When he measured it, he found it was a square, as wide as it was long. Its length and width and height were each 1,400 miles. Then he measured the walls and found them to be 216 feet thick. The wall was made of jasper, and the city was pure gold, as clear as glass. The wall of the city was built on foundation stones inlaid with twelve precious stones: the first was jasper, the second sapphire, the third agate, the fourth emerald, the fifth onyx, the sixth carnelian, the seventh chrysolite, the eighth beryl, the ninth topaz, the tenth chrysoprase, the eleventh jacinth, the twelfth amethyst. The twelve gates were made of pearls—each gate from a single pearl! And the main street was pure gold, as clear as glass." – Revelation 21:15-21

Any person currently in heaven is living there. And God's Word (his promise) says that city will move to earth after God makes everything new, at the end of the thousand years after Jesus returns –

"Then I saw a new heaven and a new earth, for the old heaven and the old earth had disappeared. And the sea was also gone. And I saw the holy

city, the New Jerusalem, coming down from God out of heaven like a bride beautifully dressed for her husband."- Revelation 21:1-2

Before this promise occurs, there will be a thousand years where Jesus will reign on earth after He returns to destroy His enemies. During that thousand years, there will be billions of resurrected people on the earth who came down from heaven with Jesus. Also, there will be those who died during the Tribulation and those who died before Jesus was crucified, because Jesus resurrected all of them too. We read about all of this earlier.

There will also be who knows how many millions or billions of angels. As well as human men, women, and children born after the Rapture that made it through the Tribulation alive –

"So will the coming of the Son of Man (Jesus) be. Then there will be two men in the field; one will be taken, and one will be left. Two women will be grinding at the mill; one will be taken and one will be left." – Matthew 24:39b-41, New American Standard Bible

This prophecy is talking about when Jesus returns to set foot on the earth again at the end of the world as you know it. The ones that are taken here are not going to heaven. All the people of heaven came down with Jesus at His return. These people are being taken to hell, as they were not saved through faith in Jesus alone –

"Just as the weeds are sorted out and burned in the fire, so it will be at the end of the world. The Son of Man will send his angels, and they will remove from his Kingdom everything that causes sin and all who do evil." – Matthew 13:40-41

The earth will then be repopulated for a thousand years by the human men and women who made it through those seven years and were saved through faith in Jesus alone. After the thousand years is over, Satan will be released to prove (once again) that men and women born with a sinful nature will still rebel against God and follow Satan. This despite the fact that Jesus will have removed war from the earth (Isaiah 2:4). The number of those that will rebel will be more than can be counted and, along with Satan, they will try to overthrow God but will be defeated –

"When the thousand years are over, Satan will be released from his prison and will go out to deceive the nations in the four corners of the earth, and to gather them for battle. In number they are like the sand on the

seashore. They marched across the breadth of the earth and surrounded the camp of God's people, the city he loves. But fire came down from heaven and devoured them." – Revelation 20:7-9

It is at that point that God will make everything new. The heavens and the earth, and everyone who does not yet have their resurrected sinless body will be changed. From that point on, no one will be able to sin because they will have the full knowledge of God. Even the animals on the earth will know God –

"The wolf will live with the lamb, the leopard will lie down with the goat, the calf and the lion and the yearling together; and a little child will lead them. The cow will feed with the bear, their young will lie down together, and the lion will eat straw like the ox. The infant will play near the cobra's den, and the young child will put its hand into the viper's nest. They will neither harm nor destroy on all my holy mountain, for the earth will be filled with the knowledge of the LORD." – Isaiah 11:6-9, NIV Bible

This will most likely mean animals will be able to talk again like they used to in the Garden of Eden. Everyone and everything on earth, along with everything in the universe, will be perfect for all eternity.

Every person will be perfected in Christ, so they cannot sin anymore –

"He will take our weak mortal bodies and change them into glorious bodies like his own.." – Philippians 3:21a

They will shine like the sun because they will have God's righteousness –

"Then the righteous will shine like the sun in their Father's Kingdom." – Matthew 13:43

Their works done before they were resurrected will be judged, and they will be rewarded for those works that benefited God's kingdom –

"On the judgment day, fire will reveal what kind of work each builder (believer in Christ) has done. The fire will show if a person's work has any value. If the work survives, that builder will receive a reward." – 1 Corinthians 3:13-14

And God will once again dwell with people on the earth –

"And I heard a loud voice from the throne saying, "Look! God's dwelling place is now among the people, and he will dwell with them. They will be his

people, and God himself will be with them and be their God." – Revelation 21:3, NIV Bible

These are God's promises, and the Bible says God never lies –

"...in the hope of eternal life, which God, who does not lie, promised before the beginning of time." – Titus 1:2, NIV Bible

The Bible says it is impossible for God to lie –

"So God has given both His promise and His oath. These two things are unchangeable because it is impossible for God to lie." – Hebrews 6:18

Remember, God said all these things are trustworthy and true –

"Write this down, for what I tell you is trustworthy and true." – Revelation 21:5

Now if these things about heaven are true, then the opposite of all this must also be true. Jesus loved us enough to tell us both sides of eternal life. Everyone will be resurrected, even those that died without saving faith in Jesus Christ. At the end of the thousand-year reign of Jesus on earth, all those that died without saving faith during the entire 7000 years of earth's history will be resurrected too –

"Then I saw a great white throne and Him (Jesus) who was seated on it... And I saw the dead, great and small, standing before the throne, and books were opened. Then another book was opened, which is the book of life. And the dead were judged by what was written in the books, according to what they had done. And the sea gave up the dead who were in it, Death and Hades gave up the dead who were in them, and they were judged, each one of them, according to what they had done... And if anyone's name was not found written in the book of life, he was thrown into the lake of fire." – Revelation 20:11, 12-13, 15, ESV Bible

None of the names of those resurrected at the end of the thousand years will be found in the Book of Life. The Great White Throne Judgment is for those who did not come to saving faith in Christ alone and the deeds written in the books will condemn them to an eternity of suffering in the lake of fire. Jesus taught that everyone would be resurrected to either everlasting life with Him, or resurrected for everlasting punishment –

"For the hour is coming in which all who are in the graves will hear His voice and come forth—those who have done good, to the resurrection of life,

and those who have done evil, to the resurrection of condemnation." – John 5:28-29, NKJV Bible

"And these will go away into everlasting punishment, but the righteous into eternal life." – Matthew 25:46, NKJV Bible

Jesus taught everlasting punishment so being thrown into the lake of fire is not the annihilation of the soul as some teach.

God is an eternal God. He made people in His image, and as such, they are also eternal. Since the eternal God is also a just God, sin must be punished eternally. There is no temporary punishment, as Roman Catholicism and other religions teach. It is forever.

However, as much as God is just, He is even more merciful! He was outside of the time and space of His creation but entered into that creation, in the person of Jesus Christ, to save what was lost. God humbled Himself, even to the point of being nailed to a cross! Because that was what it took to redeem His creation and give anyone who would believe in His wonderful and merciful gift of grace, through faith in Jesus Christ alone, another chance to live eternally with Him. There are so many other blessings too!

It is my most sincere prayer, if you haven't already, that you accept the gift of God's grace. His forgiveness of your sins through faith in the life, death, and resurrection Jesus Christ. The offer will not be there forever. And if the Rapture has already occurred…it will be gone soon.

Appendix

For Chapter - How Many Will be Taken in the Rapture

Let's start by going over the list of evidences from God's Word that a person has truly received the gift of God's grace, the forgiveness of their sins, through faith in the life, death and resurrection of Jesus Christ alone.

Evidences 1 and 2 –

Romans 10:9-10 tells us exactly how to be saved –

"If you openly declare that Jesus is Lord and believe in your heart that God raised him from the dead, you will be saved. For it is by believing in your heart that you are made right with God, and it is by openly declaring your faith that you are saved."

We must confess Jesus as our Lord and Savior to God the Father and to Jesus. Also to the people of the world, and truly believe in our heart that God raised Jesus the dead. This is how a person gets saved from God's wrath that is going to be poured out on the world after the Rapture. It is also how to avoid an eternal punishment for your sins after the death of the body you are in right now.

Confessing that Jesus is Lord means that we acknowledge and believe who Jesus was on earth, and who He is right now.

Jesus was God in the flesh who came to earth –

"Philip said, "Lord, show us the Father, and we will be satisfied." Jesus replied, "Have I been with you all this time, Philip, and yet you still don't know who I am? Anyone who has seen me has seen the Father!" – John 14:8-9

Jesus was born of a virgin through the power of the Holy Spirit –

"Don't be afraid, Mary," the angel told her, "for you have found favor with God! You will conceive and give birth to a son, and you will name him Jesus. He will be very great and will be called the Son of the Most High. The Lord God will give him the throne of his ancestor David. And he will reign over Israel forever; his Kingdom will never end!" Mary asked the angel, "But how can this happen? I am a virgin." The angel replied, "The Holy Spirit will come upon you, and the power of the Most High will overshadow

you. So the baby to be born will be holy, and he will be called the Son of God." – Luke 1:30-35

Jesus lived a sinless life to be the perfect sacrifice for sins –

"For God made Christ, who never sinned, to be the offering for our sin, so that we could be made right with God through Christ." – 2 Corinthians 5:21

Jesus was crucified, died and raised to life again –

"I passed on to you what was most important and what had also been passed on to me. Christ died for our sins, just as the Scriptures said. He was buried, and He was raised from the dead on the third day, just as the Scriptures said." – 1 Corinthians 15:3-4

So that all who believe in Jesus may have eternal life (John 3:36). That's who Jesus was on earth.

Who He is right now is the risen Lord Christ who is in His resurrected body, the first resurrected person from the dead –

"He is the beginning and the first born from among the dead, so that in everything He might have the supremacy." – Colossians 1:18, NIV Bible

He is in an imperishable body and is now ruler over the entire universe. He won the right to rule the universe because of what He did on earth –

"Jesus came and told his disciples (after His resurrection), "I have been given all authority in heaven and on earth." – Matthew 28:18

Jesus says if we do not acknowledge who He is before others, He will not acknowledge us as one of His true believers before God –

"Whoever acknowledges me before others, I will also acknowledge before my Father in heaven. But whoever disowns me before others, I will disown before my Father in heaven." – Matthew 10:32-33

Anyone that does not acknowledge Jesus as their Savior before others will not be taken in the Rapture.

Evidence 3 –

True believers will acknowledge their sins and repent. Repentance means a changing of the mind and a turning away from sin. A changing of the mind in recognizing what an abomination sin is before God and, as a result, turning away from their sin. Does not mean a true believer will not sin anymore, but they will not let sin dominate their lives the way it used to. This is important because Jesus came to call sinners to repentance for their sins.

"I have not come to call those who think they are righteous, but those who know they are sinners and need to repent." – Luke 5:32

God's Word says we must repent of our sins as it leads us to true salvation –

"Godly sorrow brings repentance that leads to salvation." – 2 Corinthians 7:10, NIV Bible

Godly sorrow *for* your sins, brings repentance *from* your sins, and leads you to salvation *through* faith in Jesus Christ.

If we do not repent of our sins, Jesus says we will perish –

"You will perish, unless you repent of your sins and turn to God (through faith in Jesus Christ)." – Luke 13:3

No repentance from sins is an evidence a person has not truly accepted God's saving grace and would not be taken in the Rapture. Why would a person truly believe they need God's grace if they haven't acknowledged that their sins can condemn them for all eternity before God?

Evidence 4 –

True believers will believe Jesus' words that no one can be saved apart from faith in Him.

"I am the way, the truth and the life. No one can come to the Father except through me." – John 14:6

Those that believe Jesus is *a* way to be saved, but not *the* way to be saved are not believing in Jesus from the Bible. And Jesus said if a person does not believe who He claims to be, *the* only way, they will die without forgiveness of their sins.

"Unless you believe that I am who I claim to be, you will die in your sins." – John 8:24

Here are the other verses from God's Word mentioned in the book that say faith in Jesus is the only way to be saved from a person's sins –

"This is eternal life, that they may know You, the only true God, and Jesus Christ whom You have sent." – John 17:3

"Since we have been made right in God's sight by faith, we have peace with God because of what Jesus Christ our Lord has done for us." – Romans 5:1

"There is one God and one Mediator between God and mankind, the man Jesus Christ." – 1 Timothy 2:5, NIV

"Salvation is found in no one else, for there is no other name under heaven given to mankind by which we must be saved." – Acts 4:12, NIV

A person that does not believe Jesus is the only way to be saved does not believe in the Jesus revealed in God's Word and will not be taken in the Rapture.

Evidence 5 –

True believers are born again spiritually, which Jesus said is a requirement to enter into heaven.

"Jesus replied, 'I tell you the truth, unless you are born again, you cannot see the kingdom of God." – John 3:3

Jesus is talking about being spiritually dead, which God's Word says everyone is spiritually dead in sin until they are made alive through faith in Jesus Christ.

"And you were dead in your trespasses and sins…But God being rich in mercy, because of His great love with which He loved us, even when we were dead in our (sins), made us alive together with Christ." – Ephesians 2:1, 4-5, NASB

This is what it means to be born again in Christ. Those that are not born again spiritually will not be taken in the Rapture.

Evidence 6 –

True believers will surrender their lives to Jesus. There are a few reasons for this. God's Word says true believers will not love the world, they will love God. And it says that a person cannot love both the world and God, which means they must choose.

"Do not love the world or the things of the world. If anyone loves the world, the love of the Father is not in him (or her)." – 1 John 2:15, NKJV

God's Word also says true believers have Jesus living in their heart through God's Holy Spirit.

"God has identified us as His own by placing the Holy Spirit into our hearts…" – 1 Corinthians 1:22

When God places the Holy Spirit in a believer's heart, Jesus also resides there too –

"God has sent forth the Spirit of His Son (Jesus) into your hearts…" – Galatians 4:6, NKJV

And when a true believer has God's Holy Spirit and Jesus in their heart, their body becomes a temple for the living God and He claims ownership over that person, body and soul –

"Do you not know that your body is the temple of the Holy Spirit who is in you, whom you have from God, and you are not your own? For you were bought at a price; therefore, glorify God in your body and in your spirit, which are God's." – 1 Corinthians 6:19-20, NKJV

A true believer was bought at a price, a tremendous price. The Creator of everything you see humbled Himself to becoming an embryo in the womb, being born just like we are. Living a sinless life for 33 years and then letting His own creation of human beings kill Him in the most horrible way known to mankind at the time – crucifixion. Jesus' Spirit was then pushed down through the earth and locked behind the gates of hell for three days before He rose again from the dead.

Jesus (who is God) did this for you and for me. And since He did, He has won the right to tell all true believers they need to surrender their lives to Him to find eternal life –

"For whoever desires to save his (or her) life will lose it, but whoever loses his (or her) life for My sake will find it (eternal life)." – Matthew 16:25, NKJV

Those who claim to be believers in Christ, but have not surrendered their lives to Him, will not be taken in the Rapture.

Evidence 7 –

As evidence of truly surrendering their lives to Jesus, true believers will try to do God's will for their lives. All true believers are part of one body in Christ but each person has a different function within that body, just as each part of a body functions differently –

"For as we have many members in one body, but all the members do not have the same function, so we, being many, are one body in Christ, and individually members of one another. Having then gifts differing according to the grace that is given to us, let us use them." – Romans 12:4-6, NKJV

So, doing God's will for a person's life will mean different things to different believers, but God's Word makes it clear. If they don't consider God's will for their life important and do not obey Him, Jesus will tell them He never knew them (as a true believer) –

"Not everyone who calls out to me, 'Lord! Lord!' will enter the Kingdom of Heaven. Only those who actually do the will of my Father in heaven will enter. On judgment day many will say to me, 'Lord! Lord! We prophesied in your name and cast out demons in your name and per-formed many miracles in your name.' But I will reply, 'I never knew you. Get away from me, you who break God's laws.' – John 7:21-23

This does not mean trying to follow all of God's commandments is a way to be saved (and thus taken in the Rapture), rather it means if one truly believes in Jesus and has Him living in their heart, they will turn from their sinful ways and let God's will for their life be done.

Those who have no desire to obey Jesus and allow God's will to be done in their lives will not be taken in the Rapture.

Evidence 8 –

God's Word says true believers will produce good works (bear fruit) as evidence they have been saved by God's grace –

"You will know them (true believers) by their fruits...every good tree (true believer) bears good fruit, but a bad tree (unbeliever) bears bad fruit. A good tree cannot bear bad fruit, nor can a bad tree bear good fruit." – John 7:16a,17-18, NKJV

"Yes, I (Jesus) am the vine, you (believers) are the branches. Those who remain in Me, and I in them, will produce much fruit (good works)." – John 15:5

"Now someone may argue, "Some people have faith; others have good deeds." But I say, "How can you show me your faith if you don't have good deeds? I will show you my faith by my good deeds." – James 2:18

"This is a faithful saying, and these things I want you to affirm constantly, that those who have believed in God should be careful to maintain good works." – Titus 3:8, NKJV

God's Word also says those that claim to be believers, but don't produce any good works will not enter into heaven –

"Every tree (someone who claims to be a believer) that does not bear good fruit is cut down and thrown into the fire." – Matthew 7:19, NKJV

"Anyone who does not remain in Me (Jesus) is thrown away like a useless branch and withers. Such branches are gathered into a pile to be burned." – John 15:6

"What good is it, dear brothers and sisters, if you say you have faith (in Jesus) but don't show it by your actions? Can that kind of faith save anyone?" – James 2:14

"Such people claim to know God, but they deny Him by the way they live. They are detestable and disobedient, worthless for doing anything good." – Titus 1:16

These verses, along with many others in God's Word, say people who claim to be Christians but don't produce good works aren't really true believers, and won't be taken in the Rapture.

Brazil and Russia –

If you have already read the rest of the chapter, you will have figured out simply by using the list of evidences from God's Word that these numbers can't be correct. Brazil and Russia don't happen to have that many more of their people doing all those things, in fact it's the opposite. Brazil is 90% Roman Catholic and Russia is primarily Eastern Orthodox, but both are not Biblical Christianity.

No doubt there will be many who disagree with that statement, especially that Roman Catholicism is a false religion. However, Roman Catholicism teaches doctrines on how a person is saved from their sins that are <u>not</u> in the Bible, and there are other teachings handed down from Popes over hundreds of years that are not found anywhere in God's Word either. Let's look at a few of the 'big' deviations from God's Word beginning from the 1500's AD.

God's Word says a person is saved by God's grace alone, through faith in Jesus alone, and that we cannot contribute anything to our salvation through good works (Ephesians 2:8-9). At the Council of Trent, which was the response of the Catholic church to the Protestant Reformation that began in 1517, the Catholic church decreed this (which is still in force today) –

If anyone saith that by faith alone the impious (a sinner) is justified (saved); in such ways to mean that nothing else is required to co-operate in order to the obtaining of the grace of justification (salvation), and that it is not in any way necessary that he be prepared and disposed by the movement of his own will (doing of good works); let him be anathema (condemned to hell).

I added the words in parenthesis for clarification, but one can see that the Roman Catholic church has been opposed to the doctrine of salvation by grace alone, through faith alone, for over 500 years. They were opposed to it even as far back as the early 1200's, when Pope Innocent III began the first of many Inquisitions that would result in the deaths of millions of Christians over the next 600 years. If the Roman Catholic church did not consider themselves the same 'Christians' as those who believe in salvation by grace alone, through faith in Jesus Christ alone – and killed millions of Protestants to try to suppress that teaching – why should Protestants consider Roman Catholics the same 'Christians' as them?

The word Christian means 'disciple of Christ' (Acts 11:26). Do disciples of Christ kill millions of people simply because they disagree with their teachings? It was also shortly after the statement at the Council of Trent that denied salvation by grace alone through faith alone, that the Catholic church forbid any of its members to read any Protestant literature. This remained in effect until 1966 when the Vatican Council decided to start calling Protestants 'separated brethren' instead of heretics. This doesn't mean, however, that Roman Catholics and Protestants are now both considered the same group of Christians. The Catholic church didn't change any of their teachings at that time, so how can they be considered the same Christians?

There are teachings from the Council of Trent and decrees from Popes handed down over hundreds of years that are still in force that make it impossible to reconcile Roman Catholicism with true Biblical Christianity. For example, The Council of Trent affirmed that the Apocrypha (14 extra books not found in the Protestant Bible) and the traditions of the Roman Catholic church, were equal in authority with the Bible. They did this despite the fact that –

- Jesus said church traditions are not to be followed if they conflict with God's Word (Mark 7:5-9)

- Jesus did not include the Apocryphal books when He said he must fulfill all Scripture written about Him (Luke 24:44)

- Jesus did not include any of the so-called prophets in the Apocryphal books when He listed all the martyrs from the Old Testament (Matthew 23:35).

This is important because many of the false teachings the Roman Catholic church promotes, like the concept of a purgatory, come from church traditions and the Apocrypha. The Bible does not speak of a place where the souls of those who have died go for purifying or cleansing before they are allowed to enter heaven. God's Word says when a person dies, their soul goes to God who gave it (Ecclesiastes 12:7). The presence of God's Spirit is also in hell as it is in heaven (Psalm 139:7-8), so the soul can go to hell and still go to 'God who gave it.' Indeed, the Bible says before God makes everything new at the resurrection, there are only three places a person can be in either body or soul – heaven, and the earth, and 'under the earth' which is hell (Philippians 2:10).

Another teaching of Roman Catholicism that is impossible to reconcile with Biblical Christianity is the worship of Mary, the mother of Jesus. It started out as the veneration of Mary (which means to set above everyone else) with the first Pope Leo I in the mid 400's AD, and evolved into worshipping her from there. In 1214 after a sighting of a demonic apparition of Mary – remember souls are in heaven or hell after the body dies, they don't appear on earth, so this was demonic in nature – then the rosary was instituted.

In the mid 1200's, Thomas Aquinas started teaching the perpetual virginity of Mary, even though the Bible indicates in many places she had children after Jesus was born (Matthew 13:55-56, Mark 3:31-35, 1 Corinthians 9:5, Galatians 1:19). Then in 1854, Pope Pius IX declared as a dogma (made it the official doctrine of the Roman Catholic church) that Mary was born without sin and remained sinless her whole life. This despite the fact that God's Word says we are all sinful from birth (Psalm 51:5) and Mary even said herself she needed a Savior (Luke 1:47).

In the early 1900's, Pope Pius X decreed Mary as a dispenser of God's grace and called her a 'Co-Redemptrix' with Jesus. This is completely incompatible with what God's Word says in relation to how a person is saved through faith in Jesus alone. In John 14:6, Jesus did not say, 'No one comes to the Father except through Me (and my mother Mary).' In Romans 5:1 it does not say, 'Having been saved through faith, we have peace with God through our Lord Jesus Christ (and his mother Mary).' In 1 Timothy 2:5 it does not say, 'For there is one God and (two) mediators between God and men, the man Jesus Christ (and his mother Mary.)' These are completely false teachings regarding Mary the mother of Jesus and are completely incompatible with true Biblical Christianity.

When you put all these false teachings together from the Roman Catholic church, Jesus becomes something those false teachings say He is not. One who is incapable of delivering us from our sins by His life, death and resurrection. Thus, the Jesus of the Roman Catholic church is not the same Jesus of the Bible.

Jesus said Himself, that if a person doesn't believe that He is who He claims to be (the only way to be saved), that person will die in their sins (no salvation) (John 8:24). So I ask you, who are you going to believe? False doctrines declared to be on the same level as Scripture by sinful, fallen men or what is declared as Scripture by the One who wrote it; the One who is the Word Himself! (John 1:1)

(If you are Roman Catholic you have been following false prophets. The popes are not God's prophets. God's Word says no prophets have been sent since the temple was destroyed in 70AD (Psalm 74:3-9). Throw away your rosary and be done with those false teachings. You can still repent and receive forgiveness of your sins through faith in Jesus Christ alone.)

So, if 90% of Brazilians are believing in a false interpretation of God's Word and a false Jesus Christ, how many of them will be taken in the Rapture? Not many. There will probably be some in the Catholic church that never professed to believe the false teachings about God's Word and about Jesus, and really did rely on faith in Jesus alone. They will be taken, but the majority will not. So what you have in countries like Brazil and Mexico, where the overwhelming majority identify themselves as Roman Catholic, will be a much smaller percentage taken than from other countries where those false teachings are not so predominant. This actually brings the percentage of people in the world that will be taken in the Rapture down even more.

Russia –

A very high percentage of people in Russia (and in most of the countries that once made up the USSR) are part of the Eastern Orthodox church. This church claims that it is the one, holy and apostolic church on earth and that God's saving grace is not given to anyone outside their church. They make that claim because they believe only their priests are in a direct line of ancestry to the original apostles of Jesus and thus, only they can rightly interpret the Scriptures. These are false claims and reasons Eastern Orthodoxy is a false religion that cannot save anyone.

There are other reasons too. The first is the Eastern Orthodox church uses the Apocrypha to promote some of their teachings, and we already read why the Apocrypha is not part of God's Word. Jesus didn't include the Apocryphal books when He spoke of fulfilling all Scripture written about Him (Luke 24:44). And He didn't mention any of the so-called prophets from the Apocryphal books when He listed the martyrs from the Old Testament (Matthew 23:35). Another reason the Eastern Orthodox church is not Biblical Christianity is they place the traditions of their church <u>over</u> God's Word, and we already read what Jesus said about those who adhere to traditions when it contradicts what is written in the Bible (Mark 7:5-9).

But the main reason Eastern Orthodoxy is a false religion is they teach a false way to be saved. They claim no one can be saved unless they are baptized and go through a process called Chrismation (only available in the Eastern Orthodox church) which is what brings God's Holy Spirit into that person and saves them…initially. Then begins the process of theosis, which is becoming more and more like God until one becomes deified like a god, and is saved. They also claim faith isn't needed to be saved, and Christ's death on the cross doesn't save anyone; that it is his resurrection alone that cleanses us from sin. These are all completely false teachings found nowhere in God's Word.

God's Word says –

- A person does not have to be baptized to be saved. Jesus said the thief on the cross next to Him would be saved (because of his newfound faith in Jesus) and he was not baptized (Luke 23:43).

- Chrismation does not bring the Holy Spirit to live in a person. God the Father sends the Holy Spirit to live in a person (John 14:26) when they are made righteous through faith in Jesus Christ (Romans 3:21-28) apart from any works (which includes Chrismation) that a person or priest can do (Ephesians 2:8-9).

- Nowhere in the Bible does it say we can become like a god. We are commanded to be imitators of God (Ephesians 5:1), but it is an entirely different thing to imitate God than to become a god.

- Faith in Jesus is the only way to be saved (Matthew 9:2, Luke 7:50, Acts 20:21, Romans 1:17, 5:1-2, 10:10, Galatians 2:16, 3:26, Ephesians 2:8, 3:12, Philippians 3:9, 2 Timothy 3:15, 1 Peter 1:9) through His death on the cross (Colossians 1:20, 2:13-14, 1 Peter 2:24) and His resurrection (1 Corinthians 15:17). They are all necessary for salvation from our sins.

So, if almost 70% of the people in Russia are believing in a false way to be saved, how many of them will be taken in the Rapture? Answer - none. And although there may be some true believers in the Catholic church that hold to salvation through faith in Jesus alone, it seems highly unlikely there would be any in the Eastern Orthodox church that believe that is the only way to be saved. This still leaves the possibility that some of the remaining 30% of the population in Russia are true Christians and will be taken in the Rapture, but overall, there will not be anywhere even close to almost 50 million people taken from Russia in the Rapture.

So now the chart probably should look more like this –

Country	Population	Christians	Possible True Christians
Indonesia	263 million	42 million	21 million
Brazil	209 million	180 million	less than 20 million
Pakistan	208 million	2.5 million	1.25 million
Nigeria	204 million	100 million	50 million
Bangladesh	160 million	4 million	2 million
Russia	142 million	95 million	less than 5 million
Japan	126 million	2 million	1 million

Now we have a total of only about 100 million from these seven countries, instead of 210 million, that would be added to the estimate of maybe 225 million true Christians in the United States, China and India. So, with 60% of the world's population of over 7.6 billion people counted, we have 325 million people that may be taken in the Rapture. If we use a generous estimate of 10% of the three billion people remaining would be taken in the Rapture too, that brings the total up to 625 million people. It seems reasonable to believe that there will be less than 10% of the world's population taken in the Rapture.

From Chapter – Rapture Has Come

Islam – The Bible was not corrupted. God's Word is the same as it has always been (Matthew 5:18, 24:35). A person does not need a prophet to guide them to Paradise, they need a Savior (John 3:36). Jesus is the Son of God (Matthew 17:5) and was the One who died on the cross (1 Peter 2:24) and not another in His place. His mother Mary was standing next to the cross (John 19:25), would she not know her own Son? There is *nothing* a person can do to contribute to their salvation and a person cannot get into Paradise if their 'balance of good deeds is heavy'(Ephesians 2:8-9). Allah is not the God of the Bible (Isaiah 46:9). Muhammad was not a prophet of God and is not the prophet spoken of in Deuteronomy 18:15-19. There have been no prophets sent by God since the temple was destroyed in Jerusalem in 70AD (Psalm 74:3-9).

If you are of the Islamic faith, God's Word says you will not be taken in the Rapture. Throw away your Quran and Hadiths and be done with those false teachings. You can still repent and receive forgiveness of your sins through faith in Jesus Christ alone.

Mormonism – The Bible was not corrupted nor mistranslated. God the Father, God the Son, and God the Holy Spirit are not three separate gods. They are three separate persons in <u>one</u> God. (Matthew 28:19). There are not many gods and one god does not make other gods to rule their own worlds (Isaiah 46:9). The God of the Bible was not created by another god and did not used to be a Mormon on another planet (Isaiah 45:18). Jesus was not the spirit born child of the Father and a heavenly mother (Luke 1:31) and He is not the brother of Lucifer who was an angel created by God (Psalm 148:1-5) before He laid the foundation of the world (Job 38:4-7).

There is *nothing* a person can do to make it to heaven and salvation is not grace *after* all one can do (Ephesians 2:8-9). A person does not need permission from Joseph Smith to go to heaven. Outer darkness (hell) is not reserved only for Satan, the fallen angels, and the worst of the worst. Jesus said the majority of people would reject the truth and they would end up in hell (Matthew 7:13-14). The book of Mormon is not the most correct book on earth, the Bible is (2 Peter 1, 20-21). Joseph Smith Jr. was not a prophet of God. His prophecies did not come true (Jeremiah 14:14) and no prophet has been sent by God since the temple was destroyed in Jerusalem in 70AD (Psalm 74:3-9).

If you are Mormon, God's Word says you will not be taken in the Rapture. Throw away your book of Mormon, Journal of Discourses and Doctrine and Covenants and be done with those false teachings. You can still repent and receive forgiveness of your sins through faith in Jesus Christ alone.

Jehovah's Witness – The Bible was not interpreted wrong. The New World Translation bible is not the Word of God and should not be used to interpret Scripture. All Scripture already came from God (2 Timothy 3:16). Jesus is the Son of God (Matthew 17:5, Colossians 2:9) and should be worshipped as God (Matthew 2:11, 14:33, 28:9, Luke 24:52, John 9:38). Jesus did not die only for the inherited sin of Adam (Romans 5:19-20) and He was resurrected in His physical body (Luke 24:39, John 20:27). The Holy Spirit is not a 'force.' The Holy Spirt is a 'He' and a 'Him" (John 14:17, 15:26), and is one of three persons that make up the One true God (Matthew 28:19).

Souls need saving (1 Peter 1:9) and at the death of the body, a person's soul will either go to be with Jesus in heaven (2 Corinthians 5:8) or go to hell (Luke 12:5). Death does not acquit a person of their sins and there is not a second chance save yourself from hell if a person dies in their sins (Hebrews 9:27). There is *nothing* a person can do to contribute to their salvation (Ephesians 2:8-9). Jesus did not choose Jehovah's Witnesses to replace Israel as God's people (Jeremiah 31:36). Charles Taze Russell was not a prophet of God, and faithful and discreet slaves are not representatives of God on earth. They are all false prophets as their prophecies have not come true

(Jeremiah 14:14). No prophet has been sent by God since the destruction of the temple in Jerusalem in 70AD (Psalm 74:3-9).

If you are Jehovah Witness, God's Word says you will not be taken in the Rapture. Throw away your New World Translation bibles and Watchtower magazines and be done with those false teachings. Do not fear being disfellowshipped by those that will not renounce their false religion. Better to be disfellowshipped than to spend an eternity in the lake of fire that was prepared for the devil, his angels, and all who rebelled against God.

Your door to door attempts to spread a false religion is leading others to hell and has built up tremendous punishments against you. God's Word says some will be punished more than others in hell and the lake of fire (Matthew 11:23-24). If you die in those sins, there is no second chance to avoid your eternal fate. You can still repent and receive forgiveness of your sins through faith in Jesus Christ alone and be sure of your salvation.

Unification church – God is not part male and part female. Jesus did not come to get married and rule on earth. He came to die on the cross and save people from their sins (Matthew 16:21). Jesus is the Son of God (Matthew 17:5, Colossians 2:9), and He was resurrected in His physical body (Luke 24:37, John 20:27). Sun Myung Moon was not given the task by Jesus to be a messiah to the world and set up a pure kingdom on earth, he was a false prophet.

A person does not get to heaven by having their marriage blessed by Sun Myung Moon (or now by his wife Hak Ja Han) and children born after this blessing are not born sinless (Psalm 51:5). Moon's son Heung Jim Moon has not replaced Jesus as the king of heaven and Hak Ja Han is not receiving instructions from her husband from heaven since he died (2 Peter 2:12-17).

If you are part of the Unification church, God's Word says you will not be taken in the Rapture. Throw away your Exposition of the Divine Principle and be done with those false teachings. You can still repent and receive forgiveness for your sins through faith in Jesus Christ alone.

Buddhism – There is a god and He is the God of the Bible. A person cannot find shelter in the three jewels, only through the blood of Jesus can one find shelter in God's presence (Hebrews 10:19, Revelation 5:9). The Eightfold Path cannot bring an end to suffering, only God can remove suffering from the world and will do so at some point in the future

(Revelation 21:4). Desire is not the source of all suffering, it is sin that brought suffering and death (Genesis 3:16-17, Romans 5:12). A person is not reincarnated over and over again to try to achieve nirvana through enlightenment. Everyone who dies, dies once and then faces judgment (Hebrews 9:27). Buddha was not the enlightened one, God revealed Himself to the world by becoming flesh in Jesus Christ. (Colossians 1:19, 2:9).

If you are Buddhist, God's Word says you will not be taken in the Rapture. Throw away your Pali Canon and be done with those false teachings. You can still repent and receive forgiveness for your sins through Jesus Christ alone.

Hinduism – The Supreme Being is not Brahman, He is the God of the Bible (Isaiah 46:9). There are not millions of gods, there is only one God (Isaiah 45:5). The universe was created in six days by God and it does not go through cycles of creation and dissolution (Genesis 2:1-2). All religions are not correct and do not lead to salvation (Acts 4:12). At death the soul does not reincarnate, it returns to God who gave it (Ecclesiastes 12:7). There is nothing a person can do through karma to contribute to their salvation, and salvation is not the destruction of the soul by becoming one with God. It is to live with God for all eternity (Revelation 21:3).

If your religion is Hinduism, God's Word says you will not be taken in the Rapture. Throw away your Vedas, Vedanta, Epics and Bhagavad Gita and be done with those false teachings. You can still repent and receive forgiveness for your sins through faith in Jesus Christ alone.

Hare Krishna – The Supreme God is not Krishna, He is the God of the Bible (Isaiah 46:9). A person cannot achieve salvation by realizing their divinity through Krishna consciousness. A person can achieve salvation only through faith in Jesus Christ as He was the sacrifice for sin on the cross (1 Peter 2:24), and His resurrection from the dead (1 Corinthians 15:21). A person cannot awaken the soul through the Maha Mantra. A person is spiritually dead in their sins until they receive Jesus Christ as their Savior (Ephesians 2:5-6, Colossians 2:13).

If you are Hare Krishna, God's Word says you will not be taken in the Rapture. Throw away your Japa beads and your Bhagavad Gita and be done with those false teachings. You can still repent and receive forgiveness of your sins through faith in Jesus Christ alone.

Taoism – The Ultimate Reality is the One true God of the Bible. He has identified Himself as God the Father, the Son and the Holy Spirit (Matthew 28:19). He is not an 'It'. Men and women are not a reflection of the universe, they are created in the image of God (Genesis 1:27). Sin is real and the reason we are separated from eternal life with God (Romans 5:17). A person cannot attain eternal life by transforming their chi into the original chi and refine it into pure spirit. A person already has an eternal spirit inside them, which is their soul given to them by God (Zechariah 12:1). And when a person dies their soul returns to God who gave it (Ecclesiastes 12:7). There is *nothing* a person can do to gain entrance into other-worldly paradises (Ephesians 2:8-9).

If you are a Taoist, God's Word says you will not be taken in the Rapture. Throw away your Daodejing and I Ching and be done with those false teachings. You can still repent and receive forgiveness for your sins through faith in Jesus Christ alone.

Judaism – The Messiah is not coming in the future, Jesus is the Messiah and He already came. Jesus fulfilled over 100 prophecies in the Old testament (Luke 24:44), and did many miracles to prove He is the Messiah (John 5:36, 20:30-31). There is *nothing* a person can do to contribute to their salvation and by the Law, *no one* will be saved (Galatians 2:16).

If you practice Judaism, God's Word says you will not be taken in the Rapture. The seven-year Tribulation that will start after the Rapture is for God to pour out His wrath on an unbelieving world and to purify His people Israel (Zechariah 13:8-9). Two thirds of the people of Israel will die in the Tribulation because they will not call on their Messiah Jesus to save them. Only the one third that calls on Him will be saved (verse 9). You can still repent and receive forgiveness for your sins through faith in Jesus Christ as your Messiah.

Deism – God's only divine revelation about Himself is not just creation. There are other divine revelations of God to the world in the person of Jesus Christ and in God's Word the Bible. God did not make everything and then leave His creation 'on its own'. God desires personal relationships with each person based on what He revealed about Himself through the life, death and resurrection of Jesus Christ, who is God in human flesh. (Colossians 1:15,

19, 2:9). Sin is real and is the reason why those who do not accept the gift of God's forgiveness of their sins through faith in Jesus are under God's wrath.

If you are a deist, God's Word says you will not be taken in the Rapture unless you repent and receive forgiveness for your sins through faith in Jesus Christ alone.

Agnosticism – What will human reasoning and sense perception tell a person when hundreds of millions of people all over the world disappear? Do not be fooled by the human reasoning that will try to explain what happened. God is real and He fulfilled His promise to remove His true believers from the earth before He pours out His judgment on all who remain. God's reality is apparent through His creation (Psalm 19:1-2). All people have a sense of morality in their heart put there by God and their conscience is witness to it (Romans 2:15). This means there will be judgment for sins after a person dies and there is only One name under heaven that can save them from eternal punishment (Acts 4:12).

If you are an agnostic, God's Word says you will not be taken in the Rapture unless you repent and receive forgiveness for your sins through faith in Jesus Christ alone.

Unitarianism – The Triune nature of God is not something that can be understood by human reason, a person should not deny it because they can't understand it. The Godhead is three persons in one God – Father, Son and Holy Spirit. Jesus is also God (John 8:58, 10:30, John 14: 8-9) and the Holy Spirit is God (Matthew 28:19). One God in three, and three in one God. Sin is real and is the reason why those who do not accept the gift of God's forgiveness of their sins through faith in Jesus alone will go to hell when they die.

If you are a believer in Unitarianism, God's Word says you will not be taken in the Rapture. Throw away your Racovian Catechism and be done with those false teachings. You can still repent and receive forgiveness for your sins through faith in Jesus Christ alone.

Freemasonry – All religions do not lead to the same God (Isaiah 44:6) and people cannot define their own truth (2 Peter 3:16). Hiram Abiff was not a master mason at Solomon's temple and is not mentioned in 2 Chronicles 2 under the name Huram. There is *nothing* a person can do to contribute to their salvation (Ephesians 2:8-9) and make it to the 'celestial Lodge above.'

Salvation cannot be attained by 'pursuing Light' or imitating Hiram Abiff (John14:6).

If you are a Freemason, God's Word says you will not be taken in the Rapture. Throw away your Volume of Sacred Law and your Morals and Dogma and be done with those false teachings. You can still repent and receive forgiveness of your sins through faith in Jesus Christ alone.

Shinto – There are not innumerable gods, there is only one God (Isaiah 45:5). The islands of Japan were not made by the Amatsukami gods. They were made when the water in the earth came up from the ground (Genesis 7:11), breaking apart the land God made at the beginning of creation (Genesis 1:9), when God destroyed the world through a great flood (Genesis 7:17-20). When a person dies, their spirit does not watch over the living from the sky, it returns to God who gave it (Ecclesiastes 12:7). Sin cannot be cleansed by the washing of Misogi. Sin can only be cleansed by the washing of the blood of the Lord Jesus Christ and by the Holy Spirit. (1 Corinthians 6:11, Titus 3:5).

If you practice Shinto, God's Word says you will not be taken in the Rapture. Throw away your Kojiki and Nihon Shoki and be done with those false teachings. You can still repent and receive forgiveness of your sins through faith in Jesus Christ alone.

Wicca – There is no Queen of Heaven, Great Mother or Mother Goddess. There is only one God and He has revealed Himself as Father, Son and Holy Spirit (Matthew 28:19). Magic is not neutral, God has condemned the practice of magic (Deuteronomy 18:10-12, Rev 21:8). Death is not just a part of life. Death was not a part of God's plan but was brought into the world as a result of the sin of the first man, Adam (Romans 5:12). Because of sin, we need a Savior and He is the Lord Jesus Christ (Romans 3:23-25).

If you are Wiccan, God's Word says you will not be taken in the Rapture. Throw away your Book of Shadows, Witches Bible or Spiral Dance and be done with those false teachings. You can still repent and receive forgiveness of your sins through faith in Jesus Christ alone.

Atheism – God *does* exist, His creation proves it (Psalms 19:1-2). This fact will be used against anyone who claims they did not know God existed when they are judged for their sins (Romans 1:18-20) Evolution did not happen.(1) A person is not the result of a meaningless process that started 15 billon years ago, thus having no purpose in life. Without God, there would be no such thing as right and wrong and there would also be no such thing as reason and logic. For a person to even try to use reason and logic to prove God doesn't exist, this disproves the religion of atheism because reason and logic have no place in evolution.

Everything in the universe, including the first human being, was made by God through Jesus Christ in six 24-hour days (Genesis 1, Colossians 1:16). God then made the first woman from a part of the first man (Genesis 2:21-22). God has made every other person since that time in the womb (Psalm 139:13). God loves every person (Romans 5:8, 8:39), sent His Son Jesus to die to prove His love for them (1 John 4:10), and wants to have a relationship with everyone He has created (1 Timothy 2:4).

If you are an atheist, God's Word says you will not be taken in the Rapture unless you repent of your sins and receive forgiveness through faith in Jesus Christ alone.

Naturalism – If nature is all that exists and a person is the random product of time and chance, then there is no such thing as the concept of truth. So how can a person know what they believe is the truth if truth doesn't exist? Only with a creator God can there be such a thing as truth. In reality, the truth is God created everything that can be seen through Jesus Christ, and also everything that can't be seen like angels, heaven and hell (Colossians 1:15-16). This means there *is* life after death, and a person's spirit will return to God after they die (Ecclesiastes 12:7), for judgment (Hebrews 9:27).

If you are a naturalist, God's Word says you will not be taken in the Rapture unless you repent of your sins and receive forgiveness through faith in Jesus Christ alone.

References

Introduction –

1. "The Christians were in the habit of meeting on a certain fixed day before it was light, when they sang in alternate verses a hymn to Christ, as to a God." – Pleiny the younger, 112AD

- "Christus (Christ)...suffered the extreme penalty (crucifixion) during the reign of Tiberius at the hands of one of our procurators, Pontius Pilate." – Cornelius Tassidus, Roman historian, lived 55-120AD

- "At this time there was a wise man who was known, called Jesus. And his conduct was good, and he was known to be virtuous. And many people from among the Jews and other nations became his disciples. Pilate condemned him to be crucified and die and those that had become his disciples did not abandon his discipleship. They reported that he had appeared to them three days after his crucifixion and that he was alive. Accordingly, he was perhaps the Messiah concerning whom the prophets have recounted wonders." – Flavius Josephus, Roman historian for emperor Vespasian, lived 37-97AD

- "I have been used for many years to study the histories of other times and to examine and weigh the evidence of those who was written about them and I know of no one fact in the history of mankind which is proved by better and fuller evidence of every sort that Christ died and rose again from the dead." – Professor Thomas Arnold, author History of Rome

First, second and fourth quotes from Top 10 Proofs the Bible is True, third quote from Top 10 proofs for the resurrection of Jesus Christ, both from Bob Dutko

2. What are the odds surrounding Jesus Christ – https://christiananswers.net/q-aiia/jesus-odds.html

3. The Odds of Jesus Fulfilling Just 48 of 300 Messianic Prophecies, Answering Skeptics, July 22, 2013 – http://bbfohio.com/oddsofjesusfulfillingjust48of300/

4. How Many Atoms Exist in the Universe?, Anne Marie Helmenstine, PhD., Jan 02, 2019 - https://www.thoughtco.com/number-of-atoms-in-the-universe-603795

This is the Last Generation –
1. http://thefuelproject.org/blog/2018/3/2/list-of-people-who-claimed-to-be-jesus
2. https://borgenproject.org/15-world-hunger-statistics/
3. https://www.usgs.gov/natural-hazards/earthquake-hazards/lists-maps-and-statistics
4. http://shoebat.com/2015/05/18/every-five-minutes-a-christian-is-murdered-for-his-faith-in-jesus-christ-every-year-100000-christians-are-slaughtered-for-the-cause-of-the-gospel-we-can-no-longer-waste-time-we-must-act-now-to-sa/

The Rapture – Recommended books for further study
- Can We Still Believe in the Rapture, Ed Hinson and Mark Hitchcock, Harvest House Publishing, 2017
- Escape the Coming Night, Dr. David Jeremiah with C.C. Carlson, W Publishing, 2018
- The Popular Handbook on the Rapture, Tim LaHaye, Thomas Ice and Ed Hindson, Harvest House Publishing, 2011

How Many Will Be Taken in the Rapture –
1. Top 10 Countries With the Highest Divorce Rate in the World, Abayomi Jegede, September 18, 2018 – https://www.trendrr.net/8004/countries-with-highest-divorce-rate-world-famous-lowest-india-japan/
2. One in 6 Americans Take Antidepressants, Other Psychiatric Drugs, Maggie Fox, December 12, 2016 – https://www.nbcnews.com/health/health-news/one-6-americans-take-antidepressants-other-psychiatric-drugs-n695141

3. National Law Enforcement Law Enforcement Officers Memorial Fund website, Law Enforcement Facts – http://nleomf.org/facts-figures/law-enforcement-facts

4. Police Brace for Dueling Political Rallies in Portland, Ask Protesters Not to Bring Weapons, CNN Wire, August 4th, 2018 – https://ktla.com/2018/08/04/police-brace-for-dueling-political-rallies-in-portland-ask-protesters-not-to-bring-weapons/

5. U.S. Has World's Highest Incarceration Rate, Tyjen Tsai and Paola Scommegna, PRB.org – https://www.prb.org/us-incarceration/

6. Grand Theft Auto is the Best Selling Video Game of All Time in the US, Andy Chalk, PC Gamer.com – https://www.pcgamer.com/grand-theft-auto-5-is-the-best-selling-videogame-of-all-time-in-the-us/

7. 7 Startling Facts: An Up Close Look at Church Attendance in America, Outreach Magazine, April 10, 2018 – https://churchleaders.com/pastors/pastor-articles/139575-7-startling-facts-an-up-close-look-at-church-attendance-in-america.html

8. Total US Debt Soars to Nearly 60 Trillion, Foreshadows New Recession, June 16th 2014 – https://www.rt.com/usa/166352-us-total-debt-sixty-trillion/

Unfulfilled Prophecies/Timing of the Rapture

1. New Testament Chronology, The 15th Year of Tiberius, Kenneth Frank Doig - http://www.nowoezone.com/NTC12.htm

2. Passover Crucifixion Dates, 26-34AD, Pastor G. Reckart http://www.jesus-messiah.com/html/passover-dates-26-34ad.html

Recommended for further study -
- The Book of Beginnings, Volume 1, Creation, Fall and the First Age, Henry M. Morris III, Institute for Creation Research, 2012
- God's Final Jubilee, David K. Goodwin, FBC Publishing, 2014
- Rapture Ready…or Not?, Terry James, New Leaf Press, 2016

- Revelation Road, Bill Salus, Icon Publishing, 2012

Rapture Has Come
Recommended for further study -
- Hell is for Real: Why it Matters, Gary Frazier, New Leaf Press, 2014

Appendix-Reference note -

1. "The observations we make, experiments we conduct, and mathematical equations we produce in the present reveal that many - if not all - of the proposed naturalistic models are implausible, if not downright untenable. The considerable number of variables which must be 'just so' for naturalistic theories of cosmology to work are staggering. Add to this the many speculative ideas about physics that must be relied upon to make these naturalistic theories of cosmology even remotely viable, and they begin quickly to fall into the realm of mere wishful thinking. And indeed, this is what such naturalistic theories are - wishful thinking of individuals who, because they suppress the truth in their unrighteousness (Romans 1:18) are willing to believe any theory that excludes a Creator God." - Danny Faulkner, The Expanse of Heaven, Where Creation and Astronomy Intersect, page 279

Appendix – Recommended for further study

- World Religions and Cults, Volume 1, Counterfeits of Christianity, Bodie Hodge & Roger Patterson, Master Books, 2016
- World Religions and Cults, Volume 2, Moralistic, Mythical and Mysticism Religions, Bodie Hodge and Roger Patterson, Master Books, 2017
- World Religions and Cults, Volume 3, Atheistic and Humanistic Religions, Bodie Hodge & Roger Patterson, Master Books, 2018

For more information contact:

Advantage Books
P.O. Box 160847
Altamonte Springs, FL 32716
info@advbooks.com

To purchase additional copies of this book visit our bookstore website at:
www.advbookstore.com

_A_dvantage
BOOKS

Longwood, Florida, USA
"we bring dreams to life"™
www.advbookstore.com